SHAMANIC HEALING
WITHIN
THE MEDICINE WHEEL

MARIE-LU LÖRLER

TRANSLATED BY
MATT SCHULZE & WINTER LAITE

BROTHERHOOD OF LIFE
ALBUQUERQUE, NEW MEXICO

Library of Congress Cataloging-in-Publication Data
Lörler, Marie-Lu, 1954-
    [Hütter des alten Wissens.   English]
    Shamanic healing within the medicine wheel / Marie-Lu Lörler :
translated by Matt Schultz & Winter Laite.
      p.   cm.
    Translation of: Die Hütter des alten Wissens.
    Includes index.
    ISBN 0-914732-23-4   : $15.95
    1. Medicine wheels.   2. Medicine, Magic, mystic, and spagiric.
I. Title.
RZ424.L6713   1989
615.8'82—dc20   89-7393
                                                                    CIP

Originally Published as *Die Hüter des alten Wissens*
(The Keepers of Ancient Wisdom)
©1986 Schönberger GmbH + Co. Verlags KG

ISBN 0-914732-23-4
©1989 by Brotherhood of Life, Inc.

Brotherhood of Life, Inc.
Albuquerque, NM 87106

Cover art: 'Solstice' by Jeffrey K. Bedrick
Cover Design: Studio Graphics, Inc., Albuquerque
Typesetting: Business Graphics, Inc., Albuquerque

Printed in the United States of America

9   8   7   6   5   4   3   2   1

Dedication

For all my ancestors and relatives . . . and thanks to the trees that gave of themselves to become paper.—the Author

The American Edition is dedicated to the Publisher's Mother Mildred Bess Buhler (1905–1983)

Acknowledgments

The publisher would like to thank the following, who were essential in making this publication a reality:

Roxanne Barrett
Winter Laite

Special Note to the Reader

This book is an examination of the ancient art of shamanic expression, and anyone who participates in these exercises takes sole responsibility for their actions. The ceremonies, rituals, diagnostic techniques and therapies mentioned in this book should be undertaken only with the direct guidance of a qualified person.

Contents

CONTENTS

List of Illustrations

Preface

This book is not a scientific or anthropological treatise on shamanism; enough has been written about that. However, in the last few years a movement has been growing, gaining strength, one in which the guardians of ancient wisdom—widely known as shamans or medicine women and men—have been inspired to make their way to us, the "white brother" (which includes all people), leaving their homelands behind.

Their appearance is not coincidental; the point in time has been carefully chosen within the basic plan of creation. It is the dawn of the age of Aquarius now that the sun has dwelt in the house of Pisces for more than 2,000 years. The turning point of the ages comes with the descending of the sign of Pisces and the rising of Aquarius. It is still indefinite as to how this changeover will be decided: Will the prophesied catastrophe come to pass, or will a new dimension of consciousness be developed? The decision is up to humanity itself, and the outcome should be determined by an old way of looking at things: the holistic view of life and its relationship with the Whole.

We are suffering the labor pains of a new age. The birth of the Aquarian child of the spirit can only be successful if the ancient wisdom merges with our modern intellectuality; if ideologies, dogmas, sects and the like drop their veils and allow Man to experience primeval religion in a direct and living way. Shamans and their "white brothers and sisters" are colleagues in the task of building the bridge to a new, cosmic image of humanity. By virtue of our own spirit we are part of the Great Spirit, the Divine, thus becoming creative assistants of the universe. Shamans who have come forth know that the time for fruitful cooperation and understanding between all cultures has come. Whoever wants to listen can grasp the new emblem, not with the rational mind, but with the heart, the only real way of communication between nations.

We can learn much from the shamans: the eyes for the Whole, the reawakening of our instincts and intuitive powers, the real power of thinking, the access to our original Source that gives us our visions. They can teach us how to find our personal place within the Whole and realize the associated tasks of healing the Earth. They can learn from us, their white brothers and sisters, how to sort intuitive cognitions rationally, with the help of the intellect, and how to give structure to consciousness.

The message of the shamans is not a summons to return to antiquated styles of living, to those of ancient cultures; it requests us to direct our vision entirely to the present, and to the discovery of our personal center, our Being. We should not wait for the Saviour any longer; we must take our salvation into our own hands.

The New Age demands work, the cooperation of each individual; it works for the Whole, for peace and equilibrium on our planet. In these times we are all encouraged to put our talents to work meaningfully for the Whole, and in so doing, make these efforts become apparent. We must bring the exploitation of the Earth, characteristic of our Western culture, back into balance ourselves. We can only succeed in this attempt if we become aware of our separation from our true Origin and reunite with this creative natural source, for whoever drinks from its waters discovers the power of inspiration. Through this personal connection to the Divine, true Aquarian baptism occurs. Then all people can find their personal alliance with the cosmos in a shamanic way, by learning to read their own fate and following their own personal path, uniting in Oneness. All can draw from this Source whatever they require and return it to the Earth as healing and beautification. Humanity can be united under the theme of giving, in which everyone will find their personal tasks or dreams which can be "danced awake," as the shamans say.

Ambition, misuse of power for selfish purposes or suppression of others, are all companions of loneliness and inhumanity that can be transformed into real mastership and friendship, when all realize themselves to be intricately interwoven into one Whole. Only then will we be masters of our own talents and realize those of others.

And here we meet the intention of this book: In an Aquarian sense it wants to be a friendly companion, to share within its limits the wisdom of the Sacred Circle that dates back 45,000 years and is revealed today by its Keepers, the North American Indians: the Medicine Wheel.

It is my personal wish to walk the Four Directions of the wheel with you as long as you read the book, and to introduce you to them as intimately as possible. I would like to give you stimuli and practical exercises that encourage you to wake up your own "dance," find your personal medicine that awaits, and share it with the Whole.

This book wants to open the circle; it is not written for a chosen fewit wants to make the wisdom public. That is the reason I have written it in such a way that it does not require prior esoteric knowledge. In order for the term "shamanism" to become more transparent, I have given a short recount of its history and meaning in Part One, in order to link its real message with the present in Part Two. The essence of the book is found in Part Three. There I construct the medicine wheel, explain its structure, the four sacred directions, the four intermediate directions, and the revelations of Oneness in the twenty sacred numbers. All practical exercises, which aim at connecting the theoretical knowledge with actual learning by doing, are based on the structure of the wheel, which I want to call, simply, an Aquarian instrument. We are all apprentices and carry within ourselves the potential of a real master. The path of the vision quest can transform each of us into a real medicine man or medicine woman.

In the hope of being able to share a strong medicine with all my readers, and in love to all human beings,

Marie-Lu Lörler

Preface to the American Edition

I would like my American friends to remember that The Medicine Wheel is not a teaching or wisdom that belongs to the Native Indians. The Medicine Wheel is the universal power of love given to all people since the very beginning of human life on Earth. It is not wisdom from the Indians. When Mankind split into different races, the Indians had the task of keeping the wisdom of the Medicine Wheel—this they did in a holy way. Now, in the beginning of the Aquarian age, a new inspiration takes place in the human heart: it is the communication of all traditions, religions, culture and harmony in the Oneness of God within. *Ho!*

Marie-Lu Lörler

PART I

The History and Essence of Shamanism

What Is a Shaman?

Shaman, medicine man, healer, magician or witch doctor? There are many descriptions: In scientific works on this subject we will find both clear and contradictory definitions. As mentioned in the Preface, it is not the intent of this book to cover the topic in a purely scientific way. But to be able to understand the essence of their philosophy of life and to share in their wealth of thought, we will have to agree as to who these people are. For that reason, the essential characteristics of their work will be portrayed and no anthropological excursions concerning the diversity of their outward appearances will be made.

We are interested in the original and unabridged *concept* of the shaman. The word *shaman* comes from eastern Siberia, an area where shamanism was the most prominent and where its origins may be found. Translated, shaman means "to heat up; to burn; to work with heat and fire." These terms introduce us immediately to the most essential characteristics of shamans. They are masters of energy and of fire as a medium of transformation. They realize that all life on earth carries behind its material guise an energy that connects it in a reciprocal fashion, with the other world—the invisible, spiritual world. The concepts of energy, heat, fire and burning reflect the actual personal experiences of shamans while they dwelled in the other world, meeting the spirits, gods or the Supreme Being. A characteristic ability of shamans is their real access to and contact with the beings of the other world, the beings of the heavens. They experience contact with that other world as a magical flight, as ecstasy, giving them insight into the original Oneness of heaven and earth—of God and Man. Thus, within their communities, they become confidants of creation and the most important mediators between the two worlds. A shaman knows that the harmonic sustenance of the community is decided by the will of the gods. On their magical and ecstatic journeys into the celestial realms, shamans are initiated into the mysteries of death and reincarnation (a common keynote in all early cultures). They experience these secrets during their transformation from the physical into the spiritual. Shamans can intentionally leave their bodies, temporarily reaching the realm of the souls because they themselves become entirely Soul.

Mircea Eliade, a man who worked with shamanism for almost his entire life, described the capacity for ecstasy as one of the earliest phenomena, because it is a part of the human constitution, independent of the course of history and forms of civilization. It was known to all of primitive humanity. The shaman's knowledge of the immortality of the soul and the existence of the other world with all its beings, stems from the ecstatic experiences he or she has with actual, if only temporary, death. This capacity was a privilege of the shaman. As the chosen ones, having access to the realm of the gods, they were worshiped by the whole community, and the shamans' instructions were obeyed as if they were voiced directly by the gods.

The Calling of a Shaman

Innumerable examples from primitive societies show that the profession of shaman was chosen in a special way: it was a calling, or more precisely, a divine selection. How does this manifest itself to the prospective shaman? Often the omen occurs during a severe illness, which conveys to the sick person that the way of healing is to drop everything and follow the way of the shamans. Another way to the calling is that of a sudden vision in which a spirit appears to the chosen one, most likely the spirit of one of the person's ancestors or of a deceased shaman, who passes on the responsibility of becoming a shaman. The call is also heard in dreams, in which the candidate, in a trancelike state, experiences the entire path of apprenticeship up to the ritual of initiation. Others are struck by lightning, which doesn't kill them, but their personal histories are erased, and suddenly their true mission is revealed. There are also examples of hereditary transmission of the position of shaman where it is kept in one family over centuries.

Acquiring Shamanic Capabilities

Traditionally, there are two methods of teaching that shamans can encounter while developing their powers. By one method the candidate is introduced through the experience of ecstasy, to spirits who will accompany the shaman throughout his or her life as teachers, special guardians and helpers. They are personal allies, who, step by step, open the other world to him or her. By the other method, the candidate is led through an apprenticeship with an experienced shaman.

The acquisition of shamanic abilities occurs similarly in all primitive societies of the world. This represents the most important steps of the shamanic apprenticeship to be mastered by the initiates so that they can finally become ecstatic masters themselves. One of the most important stages is the personal experience of their own death and resulting rebirth in which novices experience the renewal of their personalities—which can never be the same again. This is the actual start of their true mission. In this experience they cross the borders of earthly existence for the first time and reach their divine origin. The reports of prospective shamans tell us that they felt the breakthrough into the other world was a real journey that they had set out on as unencumbered souls. They were weightless and had the ability to fly; they understood the language of animals, plants and stones and met other souls.

Let us hear the report of an Avam-Samoyedic shaman from Siberia telling of his experiences during his journey of initiation as described in Mircea Eliade's book, *Shamanism and Archaic Techniques of Ecstasy*, Bollingen Foundation/Princeton University Press, 1972 (39–42):

> Sick with smallpox, the future shaman remained unconscious for three days and so nearly dead that on the third day he was almost buried. His initiation took place during this time. He remembered having been carried into the middle of a sea. There he heard his Sickness (that is, smallpox) speak, saying to him: "From the Lords of the Water you will receive the gift of shamanizing. Your name as a shaman will be Huottarie ("Diver"). Then the Sickness troubled the water of the sea. The candidate came out and climbed a mountain. There he met a naked woman and began to suckle at her breast. The woman, who was probably the Lady of the Water, said to him: "You are my child; that is why I let you suckle at my breast. You will meet many hardships and be greatly wearied." The husband of the Lady of the Water, the Lord of the Underworld, then gave him two guides, an ermine and a mouse, to lead him to the underworld. When they came to a high place, the guides showed him seven tents with torn roofs. He entered the first and there found the inhabitants of the underworld and the men of the Great Sickness (syphilis). These men tore out his heart and threw it into a pot. In other tents he met the Lord of Madness and the Lords of all the nervous disorders, as well as the evil shamans. Thus he learned the various diseases that torment mankind. (That is, he learned to know and cure them.)
>
> The candidate, always behind his guides, then came to the Land of the Female Shamans, who strengthened his throat and his voice (taught him how to sing). He was then carried to the shores of the Nine Seas. In the middle of one of them was an island, and in the middle of the

island a young birch tree rose to the sky. It was the Tree of the Lord of the Earth. Beside it grew nine herbs, the ancestors of all the plants on earth. The tree was surrounded by seas, and in each of these swam a species of bird with its young. There were several kinds of ducks, a swan, and a sparrow-hawk. The candidate visited all these seas; some of them were salt, others so hot he could not go near the shore. After visiting the seas, the candidate raised his head and, in the top of the tree, saw men (these are the ancestors of the nations, stationed in the branches of the World Tree): Tavgy-Samoyed, Russians, Dolgan, Yakut and Tungus. He heard voices: "It has been decided that you shall have a drum (that is, the body of a drum) from the branches of this tree." He began to fly with the birds of the seas. As he left the shore, the Lord of the Tree called to him: "My branch has just fallen; take it and make a drum of it that will serve you all your life." The branch had three forks and the Lord of the Tree bade him make three drums from it, to be guarded by three women, each drum being for a special ceremony—the first for shamanizing women in childbirth, the second for curing the sick, the third for finding those lost in the snow.

The Lord of the Tree also gave branches to all the men who were in the tree top. But, appearing from the tree up to the chest in human form, he added: "One branch only I give not to the shamans, for I keep it for the rest of humanity. They can make dwellings from it and use it for their other needs. I am the Tree that gives life to all men." Clasping the branch, the candidate was ready to resume his flight when again he heard a human voice, this time revealing to him the medicinal virtues of the seven plants and giving him certain instructions concerning the art of the shaman. But, the voice added, he must marry three women (which, in fact, he later did by marrying three orphan girls whom he had cured of smallpox).

He then came to an endless sea and there he found trees and seven stones. The stones spoke to him one after the other. The first had teeth like bears' teeth and a basket-shaped cavity, and it revealed to him that it was the stone of "earth-pressure", it pressed on the fields with its weight, so that they should not be carried away by the wind. The second served to melt iron. He remained with these stones for seven days and so learned how they could be of use to men.

Then his two guides, the ermine and the mouse, led him to a high, rounded mountain. He saw an opening before him and entered a bright cave, covered with mirrors, in the middle of which there was something like a fire. He saw two women, naked but covered with hair, like reindeer (these are personifications of the Mother of the Animals that play a great part in Arctic and Siberian religion). Then he saw that there was no fire burning but that the light came from above, through an opening. One of the women told him that she was pregnant and would give birth to two reindeer; one would be the sacrificial animal (that is, it would be set free by the sick man) of the Dolgan and Evenki, the other that of the Tavgi. She also gave him a hair, which was to be useful to him when he shamanized for reindeer. The other woman also gave birth to two reindeer, symbols of the animals that would aid man in all his works and also supply his food. The cave had two openings, toward the north and toward the south; through each of them the young women sent a reindeer to serve the forest people (Dolgan and Evenki). The second woman, too, gave him a hair. When he shamanizes, he should turn to this cave in his spirit.

Then the candidate came to a desert and saw a distant mountain. After three days' travel he reached it, entered an opening, and came upon a naked man working a bellows. On the fire was a cauldron "as big as half the earth." The naked man saw him and caught him with a huge pair of tongs. The novice had time to think, "I am dead!" The man cut off his head, chopped his body into bits, and put everything in the cauldron. There he boiled his body for three years. There were also three anvils, and the naked man forged the candidate's head on the third, which was the one on which the best shamans were forged. Then he threw the head into one of three pots that stood there, the one in which the water was the coldest. He now revealed to the candidate that, when he was called to cure someone, if the water in the ritual pot was very hot, it would be useless to shamanize, for the man was already lost; if the water was warm, he was sick but would recover; cold water denoted a healthy man.

The blacksmith then fished the candidate's bones out of a river, in which they were floating, put them together, and covered them with flesh again. He counted them and told him that he had three too many; he was therefore to obtain three shaman's costumes. He forged his head and taught him how to read the letters that are inside it. He changed his eyes; and that is why, when he shamanizes, he does not see with his bodily eyes but with these mystical eyes. He pierced his ears, making him able to understand the language of plants. Then the candidate found himself on the summit of a mountain, and finally woke in the yurt, among his family. Now he can sing and shamanize indefinitely, without ever growing tired.

Here the story ends. All descriptions of initiations show the special way in which a personal field of healing is assigned to the novice. The mythological and religious symbols, on the other hand, are amazingly similar. In this way, everyone finds their own allies, helping or guardian spirits, who will show them the Oneness of all life and stand forever at their side. Through the taking away of the old life of our novice in the above story, his usual way of perception died. By being freshly reassembled and reborn with mystical sense organs, he became one with all beings, above all the forces of nature, whose language he was now able to understand. Also, the new name the novice received bears significance, as it was meant to remind him of his rebirth and his new mission.

The magical objects he received from his helpers are to be antennae directed at the invisible world throughout his life. These are called *Objects of Power*. Shamans use them in their rituals as symbols of power enabling them to penetrate the various realms represented by these objects and to obtain help and advice from their spirits, without whom they could never heal.

27

Amazingly, the accessories and medicine bags of shamans in all cultures almost always contain the same things: a drum, rattle, feathers, herbs, the sacred pipe, tobacco, crystals, stones, animal masks, furs, bones, skins, shells, mirrors, coins and a ceremonial garment. These ritual instruments fulfill different functions during healing sessions.

Another way of learning that will provide the novice access to magical powers is the experience of solitude, out in nature, usually accompanied by fasting and other personal sacrifices. The North American Indians call this exercise *vision quest*. One prays for a vision, for their "medicine," asking the natural powers for a sign. An old Huicho Indian from the high plains of Mexico told of his vision quest at the Meeting of the Shamans. I will attempt to relate it here in my own words: He spent three months on a high mountain. During this period of time he fasted and talked to no one except his fire which he kept going day and night. He prayed to the spirit of this element, told it all his dreams and turned to it in trust with all his questions. By and by, he understood what the fire had to teach him. All his inner doubts and fears were reflected in entities that came to him during the night, torturing and testing him severely. But he stood firm, and at the end of the third month, the spirit of the fire revealed its medicine to him. A spark grew out of the flames and struck him between the eyes. It didn't hurt him; on the contrary, he felt it fill him with power and love.

The fire baptized him as a shaman, assigned him his mission, and presented him with his medicine: the power to heal. Strengthened and happy, he returned to his village where he still works as a powerful shaman.

Learning out in nature—by watching patiently and without expectation, by exercising instinctual perception like an animal—demands a devotion that is a necessary requirement for many apprentice shamans. Their organs of perception have to be sensitized to be able to recognize the many vibrations and currents of the earth and finally to be able to see the invisible world and its entities.

In many tribes, learning out in nature is supported by the smoking of hallucinogenic plants or by the ingestion of certain drinks or mushrooms that produce an intoxicating effect. On these journeys the spirit of the magic plant will appear to the novices and instruct them in the art of herbal medicine—provided that this is their assigned field.

Last but not least, the inner disposition of the novice is important. There are lessons to be learned every day, as long as he or she lives on earth.

Shamanism and the Cosmic Conception of the World

As we have already seen, the uniqueness of the shamans consists of their access to the Other World. Through the power of their will they can pass over into the invisible world, closed to the common people, unharmed—unlike the insane and mad in our own society who do have the gift of reaching the other world but cannot reconnect with their earthly ties after these involuntary excursions.

Shamans do not come back to earth insane after their journeys because they possess the code enabling them to decipher their cosmic experiences, to unlock their symbolic characters and let them become real, in the way required by their calling: caring for the welfare of the peoples of their community. Within their tribes they are the Chosen Ones, who speak with the voice of the Supreme Being.

In traditional shamanism, the other world reveals itself in the duality of "overworld" and "underworld." The overworld represents the heavens and the realm of the gods, and the underworld symbolizes the realm of the dead and the souls.

Where did this arrangement of the world come from? In mythological or prehistoric times, before the invention of the calendar, Man looked to the heavens with its constellations. Here the great laws of universal motion were written; here the orbital motion of sun and moon demonstrated to whomever lifted his or her gaze the cycles of life and death, out of which again life is born, and which in turn has to die. In this way it moves on infinitely and is carried by a regularity that governs everything there is. And whoever understood the signs and the language of the stars realized that the above is mirrored in the below, and vice versa. In this way the union of Heaven with the Earth, and of the Earth with the Deep was discovered, represented by the Cosmic Tree, the axes of the earth: the axis of the solstices with its two poles. The summer and winter solstices, the highest and lowest points of the sun—its death and rebirth. Polaris, around which all the stars rotate, was the gateway to the heavens. Every place that gave access to supernatural beings was designated the center of the earth in ancient times. This resulted in the identification of the Cosmic Tree as the center of the world and subsequently in its consecration. In every tree the ancients saw the connection of the earthly with the divine because it vividly expressed this through its roots, penetrating into the depths of the darkness to give strong support, and with its crown, striving toward the light with its unfolding branches! Ancient Man could still open up in trust to this knowledge of the tree; for the shamans it was the most important place, because it helped them in their breakthrough into the realm of the gods.

We find a similar wealth of thought in the Garden of Eden, in the myth of the tree that becomes the Tree of Death the instant man and woman fall from their original oneness with the divine and attain the knowledge of separation and contradiction. For the shamans this original, heavenly state still exists: The Cosmic Tree is the Tree of Life, the inexhaustible source out of which the idea of Creation reveals itself to them in its holiness, its wholeness, and perfection, and lets them participate in it through the gift of inspiration.

That is why even today we find the shamans of primitive tribes sitting in the treetops where they dwell in the realms of the gods in a trancelike state, receiving instructions and often permission to look into the future.

A shamanic journey into the underworld begins with the opening of the Cosmic Tree into the darkness of the earth. A spring, well or big knothole, one of which is usually found at a holy tree, was utilized for this purpose.

Shamans describe in detail experiences of their crossing great bodies of water inhabited by all kinds of monsters. The journey into the realm of the dead always spelled danger that could only be mastered by an experienced shaman. In traditional shamanism the descent into the underworld was almost always necessary for the purpose of healing a sick soul. Even today it is practiced by many shamans to find the root cause of an illness.

Duties of a Shaman

Why has so much significance been attached to the shamans? Have they been idolized just because they were capable of magic tricks and performing miracles in front of others? No, these are only superficial considerations. Shamans enjoyed prestige and respect from their communities because they were absolutely necessary for holding them together. They were not only the sorcerers who stood out from everyone else, but their function was embedded into the fabric of duties that the life of a community required from someone possessing magical powers.

This situation also protected the shamans. Their supernatural gifts gave them power that put them at the head of their tribe but that could be misused by them. Throughout life, shamans are in danger of misusing their power; they are never totally immune to this and have to examine themselves again and again, always being accountable for their actions. For this reason, at their initiation as shaman, they have to make a public contract in which they take an oath to use their powers only for the benefit of an individual or the community.

Let us take a look at the duties of shamans and their services to the tribe. Their skills integrate a whole cluster of professions including priest, doctor, psychologist, master of ceremonies, weather maker, fortune-teller, astrologer, astronomer and artist. These professions can all be summed up under the concept of "healer," if we recognize in the word *healing* the connotations of holy—"to make Whole." A shaman's functions are concerned with healing, with a general perspective, with the knowledge of synopsis, with the relationship of the singular to the Whole.

The starting point of each shamanic action is therefore the discovery of the root cause of the problem and the finding of a solution or successful treatment in the reconnection to the Whole, to the cosmic laws, to fate. Primitive tribes always consider illness or other mishaps as a sign that something is wrong with the soul of the person affected. The idea of responsibility for the creation of the disease is also of great importance. Shamans have the duty of deciphering the existing imbalance so the ill person can again live in harmony with his or her body and soul, a state that we describe as "health." Shamans explain to the patients (one being acted upon) that the illnesses they suffer from can be a great opportunity—if they make the effort to decipher the messages, which will show them that they have gone astray on a path that has nothing to do with their true destiny. The illness only shows them what has become of them, because physically speaking, it always represents a process that has lost its connection to the general structure of the organism, successfully enforcing its own will and thereby damaging the whole. Shamans as healers help the patients to regain their connection to the Whole; this takes place primarily on the spiritual or religious plane, but includes the body as well. The shamans help the patients to remove the hindrances blocking their view of the Whole.

The real healing work is done by the patients themselves. The groundwork awakens their own "inner healer," who helps them learn the message of their illnesses and finally transforms them into health, providing they accept the insight seriously and return to their own true path.

The many descriptions of shamanic sessions show us that the body is never the only center of attention during the healing, but is always viewed in its intertwined relationship with the spiritual and sacred, which determines the personally appropriate medicine that must be found for the patient.

Psychosomatics, a discipline slowly being accepted by modern medicine, moves away from purely physical classification of disease and the associated treatment of mere symptoms, by opening up to the intertwining connections of physical and emotional forces. It must still seem a step backward to a shaman, because the third human component is missing: spirit—spirituality—the point of contact with the Great Spirit of the Universe.

A Shamanic
Healing Session

Let us observe a shamanic healing session. Here, too, it is obvious how the different shamans from all corners of the earth work within similar structures, the essence of which will be discussed here: First, the site where the healing is to take place is consecrated and thereby made into a sacred space. This is done by cleansing it with smoke from herbs or by drawing a circle with tobacco or flour, while calling upon the sacred forces of the universe. The shaman turns to all the directions, to the earth and to the heavens, while following the path of the sun, and asks them to send their powers to the scene of the healing. This transforms the site into a circle containing the Wholeness of the universe, which is absolutely essential for shamanic healing purposes.

The second characteristic is the presence of the patient's relatives. The relatives, who constitute the social environment of the patient, must be included in the healing process (willing or not) because they are often a large part of the malady's cause.

As the next step the shaman summons helpers and guardian spirits. A drum and monotonous songs serve to help the shaman pass over into the spiritual world and establish direct contact with the invisible forces. These forces will then reveal the root of the "evil" and also the healing medicine.

The shaman may be advised to touch the body of the one being acted upon with objects from his or her medicine bag, such as a feather or a crystal that expresses in a symbolic way the transformation of the sick person into a healthy person.

Often the patients are asked if they are really willing to let go of their disease, that is, to change their lives. Finally, once the shaman has gained sufficient insight into the matter, he or she dismisses the helpers and thanks them for their assistance. Then, addressing the patient and the patient's relatives, the shaman offers explanations and prescriptions that the patient (and, often enough, the participating relatives) will have to abide by for a specific time. As a closing ritual, a thanksgiving is held.

To understand the essence of the shamanic way of healing, the following must be kept in mind: The shamans know that they can never do the healing by themselves. Only if they become, figuratively speaking, a pure channel for the inrushing cosmic powers—their tool—will the healing be successful.

Let us look at the other duties of the shamans. Their functions as fortune-tellers and weather makers are self-evident, so we will discuss their positions as masters of ceremonies—they who are in charge of conducting religious festivals and rituals within the community. As previously mentioned, the will of the gods is a deciding factor in the life of primitive tribes, and the shaman's duty is to know this will and to transmit it.

Religious festivals and rituals are conducted following the exact instructions of the shaman. In the rituals, because the ceremonies are holy, a community member experiences healing that is beneficial to both the individual and to the community. The power of the ritual lies in bringing the people together, uniting them without distinction under a common vision, dissolving the individuality and enabling all to open up to the source of life. During the ceremony each participant experiences communion with the Divine, and from this springs the force of renewal and unity.

The shaman is also needed as an interpreter of the constellations. All ancient cultures knew the importance of looking to the heavens to be able to live in harmony with heavenly laws and the divine plan. It was necessary for them to be in communion with the stars and the spirit of their age and to actualize this in daily life. For this reason they needed men and women who could understand and interpret these signs.

To better understand the concept of the *"spirit of the age,"* let us focus our attention on long-neglected cosmic processes that are surfacing again in the present.

It is known that ancient cultures knew not only the short twelve-month-long year of the sun, with its four cardinal points (summer and winter solstices, vernal and autumnal equinoxes), but also were aware of the Great Year of the Sun that lasts 25,920 years, and is testified to in still-existing artifacts such as the calendar of the Aztecs and the Gate of the Sun of the Inca in Tiahuanaco. These wise astronomers calculated that the sun traverses the entire zodiac once every 25,920 years, dwelling for 2,160 years in each sign, constituting one Cosmic Month. They also knew that each sign, during its more than 2,000-year term as House of the Sun, finds an expression on earth according to its inner context that we describe today as the spirit of the age.

The Cosmic Year, with its twelve Cosmic Months, reveals to Man the divine plan of creation containing the seed of universal knowledge. The ancients knew that Man was a part of it, and it has always been our duty to be a useful tool on earth to give shape to this cosmic plan. This knowledge has been preserved for

35

thousands of years in the sacred mysteries, and has been passed on from one initiate to the next, including the shamans.

The progression of the sun through the zodiac revealed a wisdom developed in each cultural epoch according to its Cosmic Month. The changing over of the sun (or cusp) from one sign of the zodiac to the next has always been a time of crisis, because it meant bidding farewell to the known and boldly encountering the new and unknown. And as the sun approaches the middle of the zodiacal sign, the new culture also nears its peak. From there it must recede and, following the sun, make room for the impulses of the next illuminated age.

The shamans of ancient times could penetrate the sphere of their stars. They were prepared for the events on earth; their knowledge was beneficial to the lives of their people. As spiritual guides, they have always been able to stay in harmony with the laws of their "prudent" stars.

The Shaman as Artist

By considering the various shamanic duties, we have in fact managed to define the nature of the artist. Artists receive inspiration from the source of the Divine Spirit; in their actions they create and experience themselves as creators. Their work radiates original power that can also stimulate the creative forces of the observer (provided that they allow this power to affect them).

The shamans, with all these artistic abilities, were and are living witnesses within their communities to the spiritual freedom that Mankind is able to achieve, a freedom that can only unfold and surpass the material if it provides access to the Whole. The shamans remind us of the immortality of the soul and of the eternally turning wheel of life and death—the laws of the great cycles. At the same time their abilities remind us of our spiritual decay and atrophy. For us, the uprooted, the shamans revive the paradisiacal image of Mankind who once lived in harmony, without the need of shamans. Through the shamans speaks the voice of wisdom—of the unity of life and death.

Shamanism and the Early Europeans

What we have said so far may have given the false impression that shamanism is a rather exotic phenomenon, unknown in Europe. This error stems from the suppression of European ancestral knowledge of shamanism through Christianity, which has thrown it into darkness. Modern Man, an intellectual species, has displaced himself from the natural channels which we today feel a need to reunite with in order to regain our balance with the natural ways of living. To achieve this it is essential to refer to the heritage of many of our ancestors.

Let us try to reconstruct the life of the Celts and the Germanic tribes, the Teutons from whatever little evidence there is left, and let us look specifically for facts that will prove (as we shall see) that shamanism was alive among them.

Even the words *Celt* and *German* contain hints to give our investigation a definite direction. The two words not only denote race, but also have a spiritual connection, comprising several tribes that came to Europe during the great Indo-European influx of the fourth century. Linguistic research shows that the syllables *cel* and *ger* both mean "wand." Celts and Teutons were, therefore, wand bearers! But what does this mean?

We all know the wand was an attribute of kings and dignitaries. Throughout ancient times, the wand was a symbol of full spiritual maturity. A wand signifies the wisdom of a person who is connected through the power of his or her spirit with the eternal spirit and who thinks and acts accordingly. The wand also symbolizes the axis (which played such an important role in the lives of the Celts and Teutons) of the solstices. The cycle of the sun was the great symbol for earthly life. The two antipodes, the solstices in June and December, played a special part in this. The line that connects the solstices is the axis. The highest point of the sun was celebrated by the ancients in a special ceremony: the "Hieros Gamos," the holy marriage. The power of the sun, an expression of life-giving energy and spiritual awareness, starts to decline after reaching its peak. Its light turns to the darkness of the earth until it reaches the other extreme, the winter solstice and the longest night of the year. After this low point it starts climbing, and is again reborn. In the Hieros Gamos the ancients experienced this wisdom for themselves: life, death and rebirth for which the sun set a living example. In this observance they found healing through the experience of Oneness. The seed for new life, as well as the seed of death, is contained in the "high time" of the sun and the marriage of man and woman. The contradictions between man and woman and also those between Man and God are resolved in the Oneness of death. The initiates of this wisdom were the spiritual leaders of our ancestors. Similar to the shamans of other races, their duty was to lead Man to Wholeness and health.

Shamanic Influence of the Celts

Between the fourth and the second millennium B.C. the Celts left their home in the Ural mountains together with several other Indo-Germanic tribes. The Cosmic Month of Taurus was coming to an end, and was being replaced by the time of Aries (the Procession of the Equinoxes moves in reverse order).

The Cosmic Month of Aries was the golden age of the Celts and Teutons. They were known as the "Men of Aries," and wore symbols of the horn on their heads. The mighty turning point of the ages that was approaching shaped the fate of the Celts, and the Cosmic Plan appointed them a special task which would have a profound effect on all European evolution. Their influence on the European races would become so strong that a common language and religion came into being. They were the forerunners of the European confluence that would later aid the rapid expansion of Christianity.

Only with our knowledge of the great Cosmic Year can we get a view of the life of the Celts; they left no written record—scriptures were considered sacrilegious. The constellations were the only signs with any meaning for the Celts. The Druids, the Celtic shamans, were also the astronomers. Just as in our observations of other tribes, the Celtic shamans held other important positions in tribal life: they were the philosophers, politicians, healers, astrologers, soothsayers, teachers and bearers of the mysteries of initiation.

They were the first to recognize the signs of the new Cosmic Order, and thus able to explain to their people how, with the dawning of the new Cosmic Month, they would rise to the peak of their culture, and then, according to the natural laws, decline.

That the Druids knew about the rise and fall of cultures is proved by still-existing petroglyphs as well as the ringlike walls of monoliths at Stonehenge, Carnac and the Stones of Extern. They used these places to observe the stars and to calculate important points in time, like the solstices and equinoxes.

A Druid's education was long and arduous. Only at a mature age were they able to utilize their knowledge. They realized that behind the visible form of reality, be it mineral, plant, animal or human, there was another world at work, one to which they felt much more related to because of its spiritual essence. The basis for their observations of nature was the natural path of the sun. The winter solstice was the beginning of their new year. This was the time of the Birth of Light. The earth rests during the longest night, gathering its power and fluids, to reawake with the rising light of the sun. The Druids sensed that the earth's energy withdraws and regroups at the beginning of December, and that Man during this time was left to rely on their own strengths.

During this time the Druids paid special attention to health precautions: they dispensed herbal essences, prescribed fasting and advised against conceiving children. After New Year followed the twelve "rough nights," a very important event in the lives of the Celts. For the Celts that were educated as Druids this was the time for initiation into the Mysteries. For this purpose they entered deep underground caverns which housed a so-called sleeping stone. The initiates would lie down upon it, and with the unique guidance of their Masters fall into a trancelike sleep, in which they would ecstatically experience their own death similar to the experience of the shamans. They would be initiated into the cosmic origins and correlations and after the twelve nights would reawaken to a new life—that of a Druid.

Because the Druids knew that the electromagnetic power of the sun's rays increased considerably during those twelve nights, they developed preventive methods some of which have found their way into our own customs and traditions—even though we may have lost understanding of their true meaning. As protection against this radiant energy they hung mistletoe cleansed with the smoke of certain herbs, brushed off people and animals alike with brooms made of hazel, birch or willow twigs, and wore amulets of gold or silver.

The initiation into the mystery of the immortality of the soul made the Druid a priest. Druids announced to their community that all life is an ever-changing process of waxing and waning, and that even the gods are subject to this flow. The Celts had a natural religion. There were no dogma or moral teachings. The clan and the community were considered sacred; the individual fit in voluntarily because life within the community was their expression of religion. This was also expressed by the rituals and ceremonies that were led by the Druids.

Along with their attunement to the sun the Celts also observed a lunar calendar. The Druids believed that the moon was once united with the earth. After the two planetary bodies had been separated, certain forces remained within the earth, the so-called lunar impulses that were most prominent at noon and at the solstices. They understood the influence of the moon on the growth processes of earth. They felt that the earth and moon were the carriers of identical poles and represented a power opposing that of the sun. They concluded that the earth and moon attracted the sun's energy like a magnet, and that the magnetism was especially prominent during the full and new moons. These moments were important for their study of the secrets of life.

That the Celtic Druids were like shamans is testified to in descriptions by the Romans. In these accounts the Celts are called "knowers of the trees," because they found them sitting in or under trees and talking to the Divine. This brings us back to the Cosmic Tree of the shamans which also served the Druids as a sacred bond between heaven and earth. Furthermore, the Roman descriptions tell us that the Celts erected no closed temples in which to worship their gods, but conducted their worship in holy groves or near springs and trees. Their places of worship were open to the universe and their connection to the universe was felt by all. The life of the Celts was an alive religion that saw the Divine in the beauty and harmony of nature.

Like the shamans, the Druids maintained contact with the world of their ancestors. To reach the Realm of the Dead, they would keep a nocturnal vigil at a "primordial crossroads," a junction of strongly radiating electromagnetic arteries flowing within the earth (ley lines). This energy simplified contact with the souls of the ancestors who were often asked for advice.

Celtic culture reached its peak around 1000 B.C. With the decline of Aries began the persecution of the Druids by the Romans, and with the sun's entrance into the sign of Pisces they were completely eradicated by those espousing Christianity. The spiritual wisdom of the Celts was long forgotten because the proclaimers of Christianity did not acknowledge that they were building their religion on the previously attained level of consciousness of the Celts.

The Christians did not know how to integrate the old with the new, and condemned the religion of the Celts as pagan and heretical, and were thus able to justify their "holy wars."

Today interest in the Celts is reawakening. Perhaps the Age of Aquarius can honor their achievements better.

Shamanic Influence and the Germanic Tribes

The Germanic tribes also came to Europe in the course of the great mass migration of Indo-European tribes, again under the sign of Taurus. They later split into Northern Germans (Danes, Norwegians, Swedes, Icelanders), Eastern Germans (Vandals, Goths, Burgundians, Langobards) and Western Germans (Franks, Alemanians, Saxons, Bajuwars), depending on where they settled. They too were Men of Aries, and their fate mirrored that of the Celts. Celts and Germans influenced one another and even lived in the same tribes at the dawn of Christianity.

Since the Teutons left no written record either, beyond a few runes, we must solve the puzzle of their existence with the help of knowledge of the stars and on remains that speak for themselves, such as pictographs, hilltop mounds and tomb findings. The Edda, a medieval Nordic saga, reveals some clues as well.

In cave paintings we repeatedly find the symbols of the sun wheel, the swastika, ships, spears, axes, crescent moons, spirals and labyrinths. Items befitting the medicine bag of a shaman were found in their graves, as well as trepanned skulls. All this points to the fact that magic and shamanism played an important part in the life of the Teuton.

But how?

In the Edda we meet Odin, or Wotan, one of the most important gods of the Germanic deities:

I know that I was hanging
nine nights long, from the windblown tree
wounded by the spear
bearing the name of Odin
I am myself near to this tree
none know the root from which it grows
they gave me neither food nor drink
down I bowed
took up the runes, I called;
down I bowed again and the
nine main songs did I learn,
from the majestic brother of the Bestla, the son of
Bolthorn;
from Odrorir the precious nectar did I then
drink.

Doesn't this bring to mind the rite of initiation in the Cosmic Tree? Odin hangs from the tree, the Cosmic Tree, the axis of the solstices. Here he is initiated into the secret of eternal life; his head, which is one with the summer solstice and united with the crown of the tree, symbolizes death because the sun will sink from its highest point down into darkness, where Odin's feet become one with the root of the Tree and with the experience of rebirth at the winter solstice. At the base of the tree is a spring, the source of the nectar of wisdom which presents to the hanging Odin, looking into the water from above, the realization of his own eternal existence. The position of the summer solstice (his head), the beginning of death, is mirrored there in the winter solstice (his feet), the beginning of new life. Thus the Tree of Death transforms itself into the Tree of Life and Odin discovers that both are the same. While hanging from the tree he receives the runes upon which is written the cosmic plan, which reveals itself to him.

The runes (the word can be translated as *secret*) played an important role in Teutonic magic. The runes transmitted the will of the gods to the Teutons. Therefore they needed men and women who understood this language and who could translate it to the uninitiated, the common people, for whom the messages of the gods were equally important.

The Edda also mentions the runes again:

> On the fields of Ida the gods will meet
> and speak there of a mighty dragon
> and think of great things and the ancient runes.
> And again will they find those golden tablets
> that were theirs since the days of yore . . .

The Teutons called the region of the Pole Star the field of Ida, which is the opening into the heavens as we know from the Cosmic Tree of the shamans. This place, in Germanic mythology, was where the gods held their council gatherings and was called Thing. At his initiation, Odin demonstrates to the Teutons how they can gain access to the Thing of the gods: by hanging from the tree where human beings can overcome their separation and achieve spiritual freedom in the Oneness of life. For this purpose, the Germans always placed a pole in the center of the circle around which they sat for their talks and cosmic judgments. The pole would point to the field of Ida, to the Pole Star, to remind them not to judge from a limited, human perspective, but to be a medium for the voices of the gods.

The other name of Odin, which is Wotan, defines Odin as the god of ecstasy. He is the master of the magic flight on his eight-legged horse Sleipnir. He is able to transform himself into animals, like the eagle, the raven, or the snake. His helping spirits are the two ravens Munin (the memory) and Hugin (the thoughts), and his guardian spirits are the wolves Freki and Geri. His spear is a magic weapon. Covered with runes, it finds its mark over great distances, but can also heal.

Odin, or Wotan, can enter the Realm of the Dead, the "Hel." He was the God of the Battlefield and brought the dead to the Hall of the Heroes, Valhalla, where they were served nectar by the Valkyries. Odin was both god and man, and like all Germanic deities, not immortal. He was a victim of fate like everyone else, yet he had contact with the Other World.

This is the picture of a shaman par excellence. Odin was the first man to show the Teutons his initiation. He was "Thrott," the courageous, and he introduced them to the magical qualities that can be had if a person couples his or her earthly domain with the supernatural.

The so-called Thrott mysteries, which were practiced mainly in Scandinavia and Russia but also in Germany, testify to the retention of the practice of the "initiation of Odin" by Germanic apprentice shamans. The remnants of Germanic places of cult worship, such as the Stones of Extern, in the Teutoburg Forest stand as mute witness to this. This initiation center was in continuous use from 7000 B.C. to the Carolingian era of the seventh century, when, according to Frankish annals, it was completely destroyed. In spite of this, one can still see the great petroglyph of Odin that shows him hanging from a tree, and also a vault with a sleeping stone, indicating the initiation rite of Death and Rebirth.

We can safely assume that initiates, whom we may consider as shamans, were working among the ancient Teutons. An 8,000-year-old runic saying goes:

"Uruz — Ihwaz — Ingwaz."

All life is of cosmic origin!

Magicians, Sorcerers, Healers, Medicine Men, Wizards

So far we've only talked about shamans—who then are the others that we labeled in the beginning as magicians, sorcerers, healers, medicine men and wizards? They have much in common with the original, archaic form of shamanism, but are separated from them by an essential element—that of ecstasy.

Unlike the shamans, they do not experience the actual transport of the body into the Other World. For them it occurs mentally, in the realm of imagination. They all need the help of beings from the Other World to acquire their magic powers; the difference is that the shamans become one with these beings during their sessions, while the others call or conjure them, asking for signs and visions that they can then utilize for their purposes.

A general definition having to do with the use of power would seem the most meaningful. We can derive two distinctions, black magic and white magic. When a person is being introduced to their his or her function as magical healer and is also initiated into the necessary knowledge of the Other World, he or she will also have to make a contract with these forces. This alliance is a promise and marks the initiate's decision regarding white or black magic, for healing or for evil.

Among those of white magic we can count all healers, medicine men, magicians and sorcerers who use their powers in a beneficial and healing way throughout their lives. Healers and medicine men limit their activities mainly to the healing arena. Magician and sorcerer are very vague descriptions. They have in common the ability to perform truly artistic feats of magic: overcoming gravity and flying, controlling the weather, materializing the invisible, standing amid burning flames and so forth. They keep their power to themselves, and do not share it for the benefit of others.

Black magicians and wizards not only keep their power to themselves, but also use it deliberately to inflict damage on the community. Wizards have basically the same knowledge as white magicians, but their orientation and intentions are different—building on envy and ill will, they aim at omnipotence. Everywhere shamanism or magical healing is in practice we will find its reverse side mirrored in black witchcraft. In some areas of South America, the practice of black magic is so prevalent that the real healers are almost completely engaged in repairing the damage done by it. It is also remarkable that in countries where shamanism was once prominent, the only remaining traces are its negative aspects, often reflected in superstitions and strange customs.

Today we will find almost no shamans left in their original form. The few that still exist work in faraway places, among natural tribes that are untouched by civilization. Colonialization was the first step toward their destruction, and the second step was the exploitation of their lands by the commercial interests of industrialized nations. Modern medicine also was getting progressively stronger, and was not willing to cooperate in a mutually fruitful relationship with natural healing methods, and shamanism slipped away.

But let us not lament over what cannot be changed. Let us direct our attention ahead to the beginning signs of change that will inspire our rigid, occidental way of thinking. The realization that it cannot put an end to disease slowly dawns on modern medicine; the recognition that we are indeed a part of planet earth reasserts itself, and ultimately that we participate as a Whole comes to the forefront. Here we have come full circle. After a long odyssey we turn again to the wisdom of the ancients.

The keepers of ancient wisdom call themselves the Rainbow People. They are men and women who dedicate their whole lives to healing. They are bridge builders, because they work with all nations and races, black, white, red and yellow toward a common goal: the healing of our planet with all its beings.

PART II

THE MESSAGE OF THE SHAMANS FOR THE AGE OF AQUARIUS

The time has come when the mysteries of the age shall be revealed to all who desire light upon their path that they may approach the Centre of all Power and Life. For a new spirit is within the world and man throws off his leading strings and will no longer follow blindly the blind leaders. He will accept instruction only from those who can perceive the Invisible and hear the Unspoken Word; who are filled with the Spirit and who speak with Inner Knowledge, and have escaped from the bondage of creeds and the inherited beliefs of past generations. For the soul of man requires freedom for the growth of the new age and strength to carry the burden of greater responsibilities. Therefore upon many will be poured forth the gifts of the Spirit that Light may penetrate the darkness, and humanity be reborn nearer to the Divine Image.

This is a Day of Days when many forces meet and much is shattered in the impact; yet in the Infinite Mind is the Supreme Thought, the Creative Urge towards perfection, and we who dwell in the Eternal Harmony are at one with these vast waves of Power, and all our being is given to this invincible direction of the thought forms of God.

For His children work each in their degree and the Power is transformed by the creative activity of His ministers. For there is no break in the chain between the least and the greatest. The Creative Power flows through all, and each is a partaker in the Divine Plan and gives that which he has to the Universal Heritage.

(Laurence Temple, *The Shining Brother* (1970) London: Psychic Press, 1941, 185–186).

I have intentionally chosen a quote from an enlightened Euro-pean, rather than a shaman's, to show that we as a society, are, in fact, beginning to think like shamans once again. Temple's vision presages the onset of a new era, the age of Aquarius. It is the infancy of a new development of human consciousness which is, as we shall see later on, tightly linked with what we previously described as the shamanic way of life. The age of Aquarius is the historic framework in which we must view the message of the shamans. It is the New Age, one that will open to the whole of mankind mys-teries that have been kept secret by the initiates for thousands of years. The shamans, as traditional guardians of the mysteries, lived in harmony with the divine cosmic order. From this source they received their vision, their task of stepping beyond the borders of their own lands to ready mankind for the future. They know that the spirit of the New Age depends on their support. Only now can they speak publicly of what heretofore could only be revealed within their respective spiritual communities.

Servants of the Earth

We can all feel the breakdown of our ideological systems, seemingly so permanent, the yardstick of our lives for so long. This crumbling of certainty causes many people to experience feelings of panic, fear and helplessness; they desperately attempt to breathe new life into the decay in order to have something to hold fast to. The menace of nuclear war and other catastrophes looms on the horizon.

But there are those who see opportunity in this time of crises, one that will make room for new ways of life. Indeed, it is no longer necessary to contend with the old, but rather to focus our energies unswervingly on the forging of the new. The history of Man teaches us the necessity of crisis and chaos for the birth of the new, in which the boldest utopian ideas can become reality. The vision of the age of Aquarius is that of Cosmic Man, who more nearly approaches the divine image. So speak the shamans, the initiates, the spiritually awakened thinkers and philosophers of Western tradition. Astrologically speaking, as the sign of Pisces sinks behind the horizon in the great Cosmic Month, so goes with it the theme of the Saviour. For Christianity this means giving up the vigil for a Messiah personified and daring to take the next step—one the natural order commands us to take.

Under the sign of Aquarius, human beings are called upon to pursue religion as a search devoid of preconceptions for their own divine origin. We know ourselves nonetheless to be a part of the Whole and discover within ourselves a sense of community.

The image of a man pouring water from an amphora is the symbol for the Cosmic Month of our age that will last for more than 2,000 years. The water is divine nourishment pouring onto the earth. It is the current of the spirit that touches us in our divinity and awakens us to gaze upon our own reflection. Ageless and eternal, it appoints us Cosmic Man, entrusts us with a responsibility greater than any we have ever known during our evolution as a species, making us God's earthly helper. The shamans symbolized this Aquarian task with the rainbow, the spiritual bridge spanning race, religion, borders—all that divides mankind. Cosmic consciousness demands the spiritual oneness of all nations, something that can only be realized through the altered consciousness of the individual, a consciousness that respects the earth as a living being.

The first Meeting of the Shamans took place in Austria in 1982. This meeting was the beginning of New Age "spiritual politics," whose aim was the removal of our estrangement from our natural bonds. Shamans, healers, medicine men and even scientists sat in a circle and concentrated on a single theme: the healing of the earth and (inextricably interwoven with this) the healing of Man. There was general agreement that our disconnection from our natural environs has swung the earth out of balance to such a degree that

53

we will have to do everything in our power to bring it back into balance—if life on earth is to be guaranteed at all.

The spiritual avant-garde of western thought chose the term "holistic world view" for the realization that all things are related, and that the effect on the Whole must be considered with every thought or action. This is a departure from reductionary thinking and recognizes that the total is indeed more than the sum of its parts. As we can see today, approaching the world in a fragmented way has led to a self-perpetuating process of disintegration, one that has lost sight of the maintenance of the Whole, leaving considerable damage in its wake behind a facade of feats and inventions. Shamans have never lost the holistic world view. They call it Oneness with the Great Spirit, always including Man as a part of the earth. Shamans don't simply speak of the earth as if it were just a frivolously thrown together heap of mineral particles; respectfully, they call it Mother Earth or the Great Mother, a term indicating not only respect but also their relationship with it, that of children of the Great Mother. For them the earth is a caring, nourishing mother, a living being inside a larger organism, the solar system, in which they recognize the sun as being their "Great Father."

The earth—so say the shamans—possesses a structure that is related in essence to that of the human body. Like us, it has a breath—the air. Like us, it has a circulatory system—arteries of water and oil. Like us, it has a heartbeat—the fiery magma. Like us, it has a skeletal system—the mountains. Like us, it has musculature—the hills and forests. It has glands like us—its mineral wealth. And it has a consciousness, its own thought, of which we ourselves are merely one aspect. Modern science has come to exactly this same conclusion and has coined the term "noosphere." In a more childlike fashion, more poetically, the shamans say: "The earth dreams us and we dream the earth."

Let us look again at the whole picture: the earth is a living part of the solar system which is itself just one of the many solar systems throughout the universe. Man is an integral part of the earth—thus we are woven into the fabric of the rest of the universe.

"There is no living organism inside a dead one," explain the shamans. That means that if we consider Man as something living, then we must consider the earth and its solar system as a living being as well, one having its own consciousness. One part of this consciousness is Man.

Man is the mediator, able to forge the bond between the individual and the Whole. As the children of Sun and Earth, we are the only beings able to bridge the gap between the banks of the visible material world and the banks of the unseen spiritual realm. We are children of both worlds.

The time has come for a common, mutually enlightening dialogue among occultists, scientists and mystics. A case in point is Fritjof Capra's book, *The Tao of Physics*, in which he shows how physics, having built for so long on a foundation of empirical argument, has now shown that all matter is energy and all energy the manifestation of a conscious universe. Matter appears rigid, solid to us only because of the filtering effect of our organs of perception, which have "forgotten" how to see what really lies behind the material fabric. If we could only learn to "see" again, we would gaze in astonishment upon a swirling, never-resting field of energy. Energy is the prime stuff of all life. In this form the spirit appears. The spirit pervades all life, makes all One. Man is part of this spiritual Oneness, and without us, the perfect layout of creation cannot vibrate harmoniously. The Whole has significant need of the help of Man.

Imagine the universe microscopically reduced to the size of a human body in which one part is sick, and distances itself from the general structure of the organism, becoming autonomous and not fulfilling its natural role anymore. The whole body suffers considerably due to this disharmony. This "disease" is experienced by the earth and the entire universe as well. The disease is Man, having lost our original function, becoming autonomous within the general Whole. The shamans have something to say about this:

Man must find his place within the Whole once more.
He can only succeed by reunifying himself with his divine

origins—now, while he is still on earth, still has a body. Man has forgotten that the divine rests within him, a source of power and wisdom. This is his Higher Self, or as we put it, his Inner Healer. We came here to help those who desire to advance to the source of their power. Our medicine exposes the barriers that stop Man from reaching his own center, where he knows his mission intuitively, with the clarity of animal instinct. In his Higher Self, Man is one with God and one with the Infinite Spirit. It is his Higher Self that receives the ideas of the all-one, all-knowing and eternal Cosmic Spirit. Man can only know of his duty, his vision, his dream, his medicine through this "switchboard" that links him with the divine. Only through continuous dialogue with this higher authority can one become a medicine man or medicine woman; in everything they do medicine will be reflected, medicine for the healing for their fellow man, healing of the earth, healing of the Whole.

The shamans have never lost their intuitive power, the power of "instruction from within," as the Bible says. This was the only way they could survive and preserve their knowledge. The Higher Self of which they spoke is the channel through which the will of God becomes the will of Man. It actualizes the cooperation of God and Man, in which we help in the act of creation and are elevated to our appointed position in the cosmic hierarchy. The Higher Self is superior to the lower Self (representing the whole gamut of egoistic needs and actions), but the path to the Higher Self leads through the lower Self.

This means, basically, that we must recognize the lower Self within us, with all its unpleasant aspects—weakness, deceit, succumbing to temptation—and accept it and transform it, bringing it into harmony with the Higher Self, so that then the impulse of every action will carry with it the healing flavor of medicine from the Higher Self.

Man's Higher Self is aware of the fact that entering an earthly life means carrying out a unique, freely chosen task. This takes precedence over our personal comfort, health, and very being. Man has an inborn talent for this; during our earthly stay we must perfect it—not only for our own benefit, but for the benefit of others and for the benefit of the planet. The selflessness of each individual for the Whole is of the greatest importance for the healing and regeneration of the earth.

Man's greed, the power of the lower Self, has robbed the earth blind and so disturbed its natural order that now, exhausted and sick, it must depend on us to heal it. Only a Mankind with altered consciousness can do this, one that treats its Great Mother and Nourisher responsibly, with respect, cooperation and love.

The Prophecy of the Hopi

According to the Hopi, since the beginning of their existence they have lived by the eternal laws of creation, to which the name Hopi—"to live by the infinite plan"—attests. According to this infinite plan, the Hopi play a key role in the survival of Man. Without arrogance they tell us that only through the existence of spiritual individuals or societies, such as their tribe, living in vivid exchange between both worlds, has the earth been kept from completely losing its equilibrium.

In their rituals and ceremonies they come in direct contact with the spiritual powers of life and receive prophecies that address humanity as a whole. For more than 2,000 years the Hopi, the "guardians of life," have lived on the Colorado River plateau, above the largest deposit of uranium ore on earth—or, as they put it, "a special place of power." They have always known that it depends upon humanity whether the great cycles of the cosmic year spell disaster or well-being.

Man's self-isolation from natural rhythms is a dominant feature of human history. Man has repeatedly tried to play the Creator, not in exchange with the Divine Plan but feeling a megalomaniac need to carry the world on our shoulders, bettering it with our own inventions. We could correct the inevitable mistakes, we thought, with still more inventions.

But the number of mistakes has increased so much during the last few centuries that no invention, however intricate, can correct them. If we compare the millions of years of evolution with the few centuries of industrialization, it becomes clear that humans have assumed such an out-of-proportion position on earth that we have become the usurpers and enemies of nature. And so today, having lost sight of the Whole, we threaten to blow the earth apart with our selfish actions.

Man has made the universe accessible with rockets and satellites but has gained no further understanding of it because our approach has been purely functional and mechanistic, having never reached a spiritual dimension. For the life of a spiritual society like the Hopi's, such inventions have been unnecessary, because they have never been separated from the vastness of the universe and have always been one with it in spirit. Our bond with the earth was lost through all our pompous inventions, and today we find ourselves in the midst of a jumble of problems we can no longer master.

A good example of one of our inventive "abortions" is the clearing of the Brazilian rain forests. Here the crime of the "overintricacy" of the human mind becomes evident. Man sees the guarantee of so many yards of computer paper and completely ignores the fact that the earth's oxygen supply is being drastically reduced. But Man's greatest mistake has been our failure to confine ourselves within the solar energy chain, greedily relying instead on the sun's power stored in fossil fuels. This has brought about an enormous waste of thermal energy. Industrialized Man has bled the earth dry with this ruinous exploitation.

The Hopi view the innumerable social problems, wars and natural catastrophes as the earth's response to all this. The Hopi prophecies of the future of the earth, long kept secret, were nonetheless kept alive by word of mouth, passed on from grandfather or grandmother to the next generation. Today they are being made known openly. One of their prophecies says the following:

58

When the man in the fiery red garment of the sun
appears to our grandfathers and grandmothers the last
part of the Great Change of life on earth will begin.

The man in the fiery red garment was the Dalai Lama who
visited the Hopi in 1983.

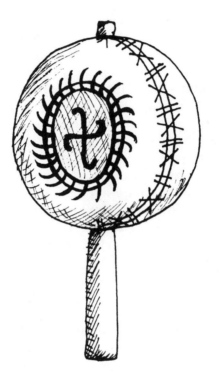

The pumpkin rattle is an important symbol in the prophecies
of the Hopi. The pumpkin is an expression of the power that gives
life to a seed. The Hopi use rattles in all sacred ceremonies. The
shaking of it is a symbolic movement of life forces. Their rattles are
painted with the swastika, symbol of the sun. This represents the
spiral of power that springs from a seed into the four directions. A

red ring of fire surrounds the spiral, as a sign of the penetrating warmth of the sun which lets the seed sprout and grow. The Hopi prophecy says that two earth-shaking events will manifest the powers of the sun and swastika portrayed on the rattleshaker. The first event will be marked by great violence and disharmony. This will give rise to the second event, which will be an even stronger destructive force. Whenever the symbols themselves become evident, it would be obvious that this stage had been fulfilled.

Finally, if human beings did not alter their way of thinking, a "pumpkin full of ashes" would be fashioned and fall from the heavens, causing the oceans to boil and scorching the land. Nothing would grow for many years. This would be the signal that the Last Event was imminent, that all life would end if mankind and its leaders did not change their course for the better.

The Hopi see the First and Second World Wars as the coming to pass of the first two events. The "pumpkin full of ashes" is the atomic bomb. They also predicted the coming of a "white brother," who would open their Sacred Mountain; however, the snake that guarded the mountain would take bitter revenge for this action. And this too has come true: The uranium under the Sacred Mountain is being extracted and the snake, symbol of energy, has begun its revenge, shaking the energy balance of the earth.

What the Hopi have always known has recently been proven scientifically—areas with large uranium deposits have an extraordinary affinity for lightning. They form special "discharge spots" for the earth's atmospheric equilibrium, above all its ionic content, indispensable for all life on earth.

The snake prepares the way for the day of the Great Cleansing. The whole earth will shake and turn red and rise up against those who hinder the Hopi (meaning all who live by the Infinite Plan). The Great Cleansing, part of the eternal law of creation, is the last stage of their prophecy, also called the Mystic Egg. In this phase the power of the swastika and the sun will unite with that of a third symbolized by the color red, culminating in either complete rebirth or total destruction. There will be wars and natural catastrophes. The extent of violence will be determined by the degree of inequality among nations and with nature. The deciding factor will be Man.

A Hopi delegation attended the Meeting of the Shamans to draw our attention to this crisis. They emphasized that the only chance of avoiding this "cleansing" is the understanding that all must battle for the One, the Whole, so that all may survive. Man can only come to grips with the violence we have inflicted upon the Earth if the consciousness of all nations changes—especially that of the "superpowers." Reunited, we must cease our ruthless exploitation and one-sided extractions of raw materials from the earth, and cease viewing it as nothing more than a lifeless stockpile. Our cold, mechanical way of acting finds its peak expression with the gargantuan expansion of our "defense" systems.

> True peace can descend only if we depart from a society based on violence in which one forces his own will on the other. We must reunite ourselves spiritually with our brothers and sisters, and with all our "relatives," the creatures of nature; we must let the Eternal Spirit rule on earth. The Whole needs the vision of every individual entity, be it stone, plant, animal or human. The concern for all living things will then far surpass self-interest, and will bring greater happiness than ever before possible. Then all beings will enjoy lasting harmony.*

With this vision of a Hopi grandfather we turn to our actual work.

*The quotes given here are from speeches, personal conversations and from the brochure, *The Essence of the Hopi Prophecy* published by the Society for Endangered Peoples.

PART III

THE WHEEL OF REVELATION

This section of the book describes the essentials of the ancient wisdom which date back 45,000 years into the early Stone Age. We will see how this knowledge was passed down through the ages to be revealed today by its keepers, the Indians. The sections are arranged in such a way as to introduce the reader to this wisdom in consecutive steps, and leave you time and leisure to gain your own experience, which becomes possible only if you take the initiative to let yourself be touched. The Indians have no written record of their knowledge because it was a part of their daily rituals and ceremonies and was handed down from generation to generation in this way.

The revelation of the ancient wisdom shows us a way available to everyone and will certainly bring light and power to us seekers once we have opened up to our personal search for our origin. It is the way of the true religion, out of which all the dogmas were born. The primordial religion contains the Whole; it is the primeval language of the Natural.

On this path the seekers will find no Masters or Gurus who will lead and guide them in the usual way. This is a path among friends who benefit each other in their solitary journey through the mutual sharing of their discoveries. At the beginning, everyone decides whether to walk the path or not. Seekers have to know that it has to be walked alone, for only in aloneness will we become free and responsible. In our aloneness we will find our center of power revealed to us as an empty vessel that is continuously being filled with the creative wealth of the divine. On this path we can find our true and rational position on earth. This center is our "Cosmic Tree" or "earth-sky axis."

In our center, we are in connection with everything in the All-Oneness. Whosoever will travel on this path will have the power of love as a constant companion that stands above all knowledge and is the source of all life. For this reason the Indians call it the path of the heart. Once we have experienced this power of love without outer influences or sex we will know with a certainty beyond any rational reasoning that aloneness is "All-Oneness." We are one with everything, one with the Whole; we are the Whole.

The true power of love comes as a flashlike recognition or in a crystal-clear vision that unites our small spirit with the all-encompassing Great Spirit. We can share this love only in our center, when everything in us is empty and silent and our surrender to this nothingness is undisturbed by any expectation. Love is silently present like the center of a circle or the hub of a wheel. It is the "I Am," an eternal presence in the fickleness of life.

In order for this book to be a helping friend, there are two shamanic rules to begin with: "Have no expectations" and "don't judge and compare." It is probably helpful to encounter the many pages of this book as empty pages, because clinging to the known through judging and comparing them will leave no room for a true inner meeting to happen. It is invaluable to dive fully into the childlike power of innocence and trust and to be able to really open up to the new so it can be experienced in its living wholeness. Only if we let go of the old and become truly empty can the new enter into us. This will be a real surrender.

The ancient wisdom always presents itself as a circle or in the shape of a wheel, the symbol of the Whole. The Indians called it the "medicine wheel." The healing power of the medicine wheel is its constant connection to the Whole. Whoever collaborates with its medicine will always find healing for wounds or sorrows: physical, psychological and spiritual. The "dance with the wheel" will lead us to "magic life," which is an awareness of the oneness of both the visible and the invisible world.

Magic is a human experience. We will perceive it if we are totally intuitive, act with an instinctlike impulse and realize how the forces stream into us without any personal effort. We know these powers from dangerous situations when we are forced to react with absolute confidence. Magic shows us that nothing is done by us alone but everything will be created through us if we realize that we are receivers and not creators. We encounter magic every night when, in deep sleep, we become again the growing embryo in the body of the Great Mother. In our dreams our spirit expresses itself in innumerable ways to show us that this presently adopted way of life is only one among many. We encounter magic in our "lightbodies," those swirls of energy called chakras which are located within and around our bodies. Our magic Self makes us aware of our manifold relationships with the world. It shows us where our "four shields are dancing" as it is expressed in the language of the medicine wheel, and, finally, magic is love.

You cannot learn magic by method. There are only the ingredients of a recipe that you will have to mix and prepare for yourself without instructions. The twenty sacred powers of the medicine wheel are the ingredients, as well as the tools and basic structure that all people can use in their own personal way. A wealth of possibilities arise out of this work, and if it doesn't become rigid but remains constantly fluid, it could unexpectedly reveal the divine to the "dancer of the wheel."

The work and the concern with the medicine wheel is the fourfold path to our alliance with God. The dance through the wheel also leads us to our helpers in the universe, who do not merely accompany us as mute guardian angels but wait for communication. They want to be invited to help us. The medicine wheel will help us to find our personal medicine. This can happen in four different ways, and these are symbolized in the cross that everyone chose to carry in this lifetime to be able to assist the Whole according to our fate.

THE MEDICINE WHEEL

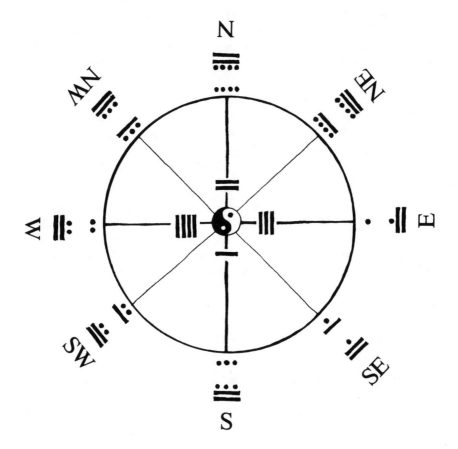

The Story of Creation in the Ancient Religion

In the beginning and the end, beyond time and space, as eternally existing nothingness and origin that contains all possibilities of life, as emptiness and source is "Wakan"—our ancient female ancestor, the original female from which everything is born. Wakan is the circle, the "All," is that which rests in itself, the receiving.

Wakan changes continuously into "Skwan" who is our ancient grandfather, the original male. He is the source, the holy creation. Skwan is a spiral, the active, the creative and corresponds to the Milky Way.

Wakan and Skwan love each other. Skwan gives his semen to Wakan and the fruit of their love creates all life. Their holy marriage bears two children: Sun and Earth.

Their first child is the Sun, our Great Father. The sacred number One, the power of the east, the power of enlightenment, the power of vision, the power of fire and lightning.

Their second child is the Earth, the world of minerals. She is our Great Mother, the sacred number Two, the power of the west, the power of transformation, the power of intuition and introspection, the power of magic death and darkness. Our Great Father and our Great Mother also love each other. Out of their love, life on earth is born.

● ● ●

Their first child is the realm of the plants, the sacred number Three which is the power of south, of innocence and trust, the power of harmony and emotion, the power of all waters and the power of the moon.

● ● ● ●

Their second child is the realm of the animals, the sacred number Four, the power of north, the power of instinctive action, of logic and mind, of knowledge, the power of the stars, air and wind.

━━━━

Their third child is the realm of Humankind, the sacred number Five, the southern center of the circle, the power of touch, of language and communication. Minerals, plants, animals and human beings are related as siblings, mutual children of the earth. They form the Great Family.

The center of creation is Humankind, the sacred five on its way to becoming Whole: the sacred Twenty.

Four elements are grouped around us: the fire of the east, the water of the south, the earth of the west, and the air of the north. The power of love gives us the ability to merge with these four relatives in the four powers of the intermediate directions.

●
━━━━

Through the marriage of the sacred Five with the sacred One, the sun, we are positioned in the world of the sacred Six in the southeast of the Wheel of Creation. It is the world of our ancestors, the world of our previous incarnations, the world of history.

● ●
━━━━

If the sacred Five merges with the sacred Two, the earth, we will become one with the world of the sacred Seven in the southwest of the circle. This is the realm of dreams.

If we as the sacred Five merge with the sacred Three, the power of the plants in the northwest of the circle, we will enter into the realm of the sacred Eight, the world of infinitely finite circles, the world of the Great Laws.

And in the merger of the sacred Five with the world of the sacred Four, the power of the animals in the northeast of the circle, the holy Nine opens up to us, the power of all energy impulses, the power of movement.

And finally in the oneness of the sacred Five with its mirror reflection, the power of Humankind, we will be positioned in the northern center of the circle and become the sacred Ten, the realm of our Higher Self.

Through the power of our Higher Selves, we are able to contact eight further powers that accompany the first ones like higher octaves.

Through the encounter of the Higher Self with the sun in the east, the sacred Eleven opens up to us, the spirit of all suns.

Through the encounter of the Higher Self with the earth in the west, the sacred Twelve opens up to us, the spirit of all planets.

In the encounter of the Higher Self with the plants in the south, the sacred Thirteen opens up to us, the spirit of the plants.

Through the encounter of the Higher Self with the animals in the north, the sacred Fourteen opens up to us, the spirit of the animals.

And when the Higher Self encounters the world of human beings, it will enter the realm of humanity as a species and will meet Humankind in the cosmos, facing east from the center of the circle, the location of the sacred Fifteen.

If the Higher Self merges with the power of the ancestors in the southeast, the world of the sacred Sixteen will be open to us, the world of the enlightened and the avatars.

If the Higher Self merges with the power of the dreams in the southwest, the world of the sacred Seventeen will be open to us, the world of the guardians of dreams, the kachinas.

If the Higher Self merges with the power of the great cycles in the northwest, it will open the world of the sacred Eighteen, the world of the lawmakers and keepers of fate.

If the Higher Self merges with the power of movement in the northeast, it will open the world of the holy Nineteen, the world of the great movers, the primeval cosmic powers.

And in the merger of the Higher Self with the higher self of all others, the sacred Twenty will be available to us in the western part of the circle, the power of the great spirit "Wakantanka," the power of perfection and Oneness.

Through the power of the sacred Twenty, We are again one with the origin, one with the Oneness of Wakan and Skwan.

This story of creation from the early Stone Age reveals the source of all religion. If we return to this source we can again connect ourselves with the healing and unifying powers of the universe. These place us in the right relationship to the Whole. This place is our own center in which we are the children of the earth and the sun, and live in harmony with the visible and the invisible. The people of the early Stone Age still experienced themselves as an integral part of the family of creation amidst their relatives: the stones, plants and animals. These relationships allowed them access to all the other powers of the circle.

That the primeval religion is being revealed today by its keepers, the Indian shamans, should not be misinterpreted as a super-imposition of the Indian philosophy of life onto our culture. The Indians only had the duty to keep the ancient wisdom for human-ity and to pass it on when the time was right. Originally, in the epoch of the early Stone Age, it was not only an Indian wisdom but common knowledge for the people of the time.

In the early religion, the story of creation employs the image of the circle, which possesses the power to cleanse all dogmatic religions of their false and incomplete doctrines. This true religion represents the intact power of reality for us who live in the sepa-rateness and tensions of innumerable contradictions. It is also the most natural way to explore for ourselves our personal relation-ship with the Whole and to discover our origin without precon-ceived dogmas. Religions that set up dogmas have always needed to rationally explain and prove their teachings. Very soon it becomes apparent that many things cannot be understood rationally and belief is demanded. History teaches us how much damage was done by this. Just think about the Inquisition or the Crusades.

If we tried to comprehend the early Stone Age wisdom and the circle of the twenty sacred powers of the universe with only the help of the rational mind, we would fall back into dogmatic religion and would be unable to honor its universality and therefore never experience Oneness. Only when we start to reawaken the fourfold powers of our consciousness will we be able to live in harmony with these forces. These four powers, or paths, mark our relationship with reality and enable us to be centered within ourselves. The four paths are:

- The path of the east with the power of the spirit
- The path of the west with the power of the will
- The path of the south with the power of the emotions
- The path of the north with the power of thinking

Each one is considered sacred because it heals and leads us to the Whole.

The medicine wheel was not born out of the power of mind alone. Its birth has to be understood within the context of a human consciousness that was still functioning in its wholeness and was not yet diversified. Today, therefore, the medicine wheel represents a medicine that can help us to become whole and completely unfold our consciousness. It is a medicine to treat our dislocation from the Whole and to reconnect the two halves of our brain: the left hemisphere that carries our sensory data and governs the waking state and the right hemisphere that produces the dreams and governs the instincts.

The medicine wheel lifts the two "homines" of evolution to a new plane of consciousness by bringing together "Homo fabians" and "Homo sapiens" in the resulting "Homo divinians." For more than 100,000 years we lived as Homo fabians, toolmaking animals, with both halves of the brain in harmony. Waking and dreaming were one, and through our instincts we were embedded in nature. A mostly silent people, we scarcely used language to make the imaginary world and visions available to others. Then, in the mythological Fall, Homo sapiens appeared; we were expelled from the Garden of Eden, and began living in the separateness of both halves of the brain. The religion of our early Stone Age ancestors was forgotten and was replaced by culture-specific, developing religions that were documented in written dogmas that bound everyone. Inventions like reading and writing hurried these developments, and today we know the Homo sapiens as the ones who are imprisoned by their technical philosophy of life, and who think that they will understand reality through the power of their linear thinking.

At the dawn of the Age of Aquarius, the dawn of planetary thinking, Homo divinians appear in the world with the mission to harmonize the manifold diversity of life with the Whole. Because the keepers of the Stone Age wisdom, the North American Indian, had no scriptures and therefore skipped the epoch of the Homo sapiens, the heritage of the medicine wheel could remain pure, and they were able to keep magical shamanism as their religion. The step back into the Stone Age is necessary because it is our only chance to rekindle the lost power of our instincts, the power that we need to be a meaningful cell within the cosmic metabolism.

The Medicine Wheel

The twenty sacred powers of the medicine wheel are the gates that make the experience of Oneness possible for all humans. Some gates are visible and some are invisible, but both will show us reality in its completeness if they are opened.

The medicine wheel is Humankind, the potentiality of the Divine which is already given to us here on earth if we are ready to serve the wisdom. The focal point is the development of our consciousness from the sacred Five to the sacred Twenty. That's why we are not interested in the meaning of the particular powers by themselves but only in their relationship to human consciousness.

In ancient wisdom the number twenty always played a significant part. To explain this number the Indians draw attention to the ten fingers of our hands and the ten toes of our feet. What does this mean? Let us remember the two halves of the brain. The right half represents the world of possibilities, the dreams and instincts, and the left half is the realm of our sensory data, the waking state. If we put the palms of our hands together, or the soles of our feet, we symbolically connect both halves of our body whose left half is governed by the right side of the brain and vice versa. Our hands folded in prayer represent our dwelling in the sacred Ten, our Higher Self, which helps us to commune with the Highest Being. The five as the number for human beings is obvious. We have five sense organs, and we consist of five extremities: the head, both arms and both legs. If we draw an abstract figure of a human body and connect these extremities with lines we will get a pentacle, a symbol for the human form. The cosmic energy flows through our bodies according to the pentacle, charging our left half negative, our right half positive, and reversing in the head.

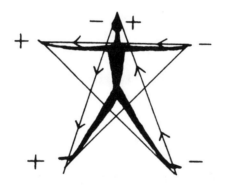

It is important for us to invoke these twenty powers out of their realm of possibility, where they are always present, through calling and inviting them and asking for their cooperation. We also need to learn to be receptive to them so we can recognize them in our daily lives. And, finally, we will have to understand the images, visions, thoughts and emotions that come to us from these forces as personalized messages which help us to joyfully accept and fulfill our fate.

The Twenty Sacred Numbers

Again we start with the empty circle, the zero, the nothing, which already contains all the possibilities of being. In the language of the Indians this primal source is "Wakan," the primeval mother who gives birth to all life. The primary female energy is continuously transformed into male energy and is symbolized by a spiral. In Indian languages it is called "Skwan." These two elementary and bipolar powers are also known as Yin and Yang. They are in harmony as a unit, dwell in a resting equilibrium and are one—a whole without contradictions. We can call them our great-grandparents.

What does that mean for us? This loving power is the very source from which each individual receives the fullness of life. This love force is not something outside our being but constitutes our actual center. When we are in a state of total surrender, it can be perceived as the silence in the temple of God. The medicine wheel shows us the four gates of human consciousness which are positioned as the sacred Five, Ten, Fifteen and Twenty around the perimeter of the circle. These are the four states of consciousness where we find access to the power of the center: the Oneness of male and female energy.

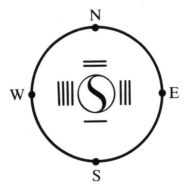

• As the sacred Five we open ourselves to the center through the gate of the south, supported by the power of innocence and trust.

• As the sacred Ten we open ourselves to the center through the gate of the north, supported by the power of the integrated mind and instinctlike knowing.

• As the sacred Fifteen we open ourselves to the center through the gate of the east, supported by the power of inspiration and vision.

• As the sacred Twenty we open ourselves to the center through the gate of the west, supported by the power of death, the transformer and source of all life, and by the power of intuition and introspection.

The way to slowly open these gates for ourselves will be shown through working with the sacred circle. The love and holy marriage between our primary Mother and Father create two powers basic for the entire growth process: the Sun and the Earth. These are their children, and our primordial parents.

The Power of the Sun

The sun is the sacred number One. His is the place of the east and the power of the east, for it is here he rises. The early Stone Age people thought themselves to be children of the sun and therefore called him their "Great Father" or "Great Grandfather." The sun's light conquers the darkness of night in the morning, therefore constituting the power of enlightenment, revelation, inspiration and visions.

The sun's eternally burning fire teaches us that light or fire can only remain "alive" through the "death" of the burning substance. Translated into our earthly existence, this means that we will have to learn to become empty again and again, to depart from the old and let go of what we cling to so we can receive our personal vision. Our creativity will be kindled and nurtured with every sunrise and we will find fulfillment in our mission in life.

Without the sun's energy there would be no life on earth. For the most part we perceive the power of the sun only materially. We either enjoy its warmth, suffer its heat or freeze in its absence. We know its power psychologically; we feel easier and lighter on sunnier days than on overcast days.

But do we know the spiritual power of the sun? Let us try to answer this question the Indian way by watching nature. Every day the sun appears in the east to pour its light over what has been hidden by the dark of the night. Let us take this image and project it on our spirit: The power of the sun's light inspires our spirit and gives us light where we were roaming in darkness. Most people live with the unshakable trust that the sun will rise again every morning, but do we know this trust on a spiritual plane? There we have very little trust that we will be so guided every day. Often this mistrust is so strong that we lose the awareness of the actual sunshine. But sometimes the "fire of the east," the sun, can spark our spirit unexpectedly as if it were hit by lightning. We all know the expression "struck by lightning" from many legends of holy people where a sudden vision gave them a deep insight into the Divine. Often these visions were quite unspectacular; nonetheless, they helped those who experienced them gather the trust and courage needed to let themselves be guided by the Divine power.

It is very important and helpful to remember our spiritual relationship with the sun, our "Great Father," whom we can ask for help when we are unseeing and confused. Perhaps we will have to become more modest and understand that not all ideas and notions arise from within ourselves, but that each of them is a sun ray carrying a message from the cosmic realm of ideas.

The Power of the Earth

The second child of the primeval mother and the primeval father is the earth, the sacred number Two. In her lives the element earth, the world of the minerals. The earth—the stones, the sand, the rock and all minerals—stores energy. She is not only able to freeze the power of energy, but she can also release it.

In the medicine wheel, the earth stands in the west as the opposite to the east. It is where the sun sets and has its light transformed into power. The earth receives the light of the sun and stores it in its dark depths where it forms a permanent and consistent potential of power. Because we are not only the children of the sun but also the children of the earth, the "Great Mother" lets us participate in this accumulated resource. The earth's gravity is like an umbilical cord that pulls from below to hold us to the surface. Her power nourishes us like that of the sun but has a different quality. She rules the human will which knows only "yes" or "no." The earth as the sacred Two teaches us about the twofoldedness of the opposites and demands decision. The sunlight that is received by the earth is transformed into images by her reservoir of power, which is given to whoever takes the trouble to descend into their own depths with the intention of discovering their source of power. There we will find the power of imagination and intuition enabling us to live under the guidance of the inner. If we act out of clear decisions, our actions will carry the flavor of truth and magic because their impulses will arise out of our center which in turn is nourished by Mother Earth.

If we are in our center, a current of power can flow freely to the center of the earth and its power will always support our actions. This is what we have called magic. For this reason the west is called the place of magic in the medicine wheel. The quality of the west as a place of healing is closely linked to these magical associations because magical healing is the only true way of healing and because disease is controlled by the will of the person. Expressed in shamanic words this means that an ill person subconsciously wants the disease because he or she needs to learn something particular from it. They can only be healed by recognizing the lesson of the illness and by then deciding to let go of the disease. This is a requirement for our return to the center. Disease finally means that one has lost the way, and visionless, cannot realize his or her mission.

The earth represents the physical that is governed in its growth by the change of birth and death. To truly grow we will have to die a small death every day to be able to unfold whatever talents are given to us. We will have to learn to leave behind the things that we cling to that block us in our process of becoming whole.

East and west stand opposite each other. The sun gives light, and the earth receives it to transform it into power. For us this means that in the light of the sun we experience our spirit and through the power of the earth we experience our body. Our spirit is nourished by the sun through visions, ideas, imagination and creativity. The earth nourishes our body via our senses, breath and metabolism. This translates into the experience of a constant rebirth in the relationship of our spirit to the sun and constant death in our earth-body relationship.

We stand between heaven and earth, between spirit and body, and our soul helps us as mediator or connector. Through the soul, human beings can embody the spirit by realizing our inspiration, ideas and visions on earth, by giving them form. We can spiritualize this body by making it the receptacle into which the cosmic wealth of ideas pours.

The soul is the bridge between body and spirit, heaven and earth, and only in this function does it have meaning in life. This bridge can lead us back into the Oneness of Being and the medicine wheel can lead us again onto this bridge. If we understand the soul as a bridgehead between east and west, we will experience it as our center, as the immortal, as God.

The Upanishads, the oldest scriptures on earth, say:

> *He who lives on the earth,*
> *but is not of the earth;*
> *who is not known by the earth,*
> *but has the body of earth,*
> *who rules the earth from within,*
> *he is the Self, the inner guide,*
> *the immortal Self.*

Neither the body nor the earth knows the immortal, but the immortal knows the mortal and rules it from within.

The Realm of the Plants

Sun and Earth, our Great Parents, love each other and their love produces growth on earth. Their love creates three worlds: the realm of the plants, the realm of the animals and the realm of human beings.

Their first child is the realm of the plants. It is the sacred number Three: the grass, the bushes, trees and flowers. Theirs is the southern position in the medicine wheel. Every day the sun travels through the south, its highest point, on the daily path. From there his light shines strongest on the earth. At noon he is halfway between east and west. We can call noon the mediator between east and west, between body and spirit; as such it represents the world of the soul.

But what is the connection between plants and soul? To comprehend what they have in common it is helpful to look at the life of the plants: Every plant is born out of the seed of a plant that lived before, one that had to die to give new seeds, new life. This seed is hidden at first in the darkness of the earth. The penetrating sunlight and the nutritive substances within the seed cause it to sprout until it is strong enough to penetrate the earth's surface. Consequently, its leaves will unfold and they will absorb sunlight to help it grow. Plants have linear growth along their earth-heaven axis. In their constant urge to grow they open themselves to the light of the sun and the sky. A plant will recognize its true parents as sun and earth, who will nurture it carefully, and on whom it can rely like an innocent child. For this reason the south represents the power of innocence and trust.

From this we can see how important it is to recognize our essential needs and desires. We will have to awaken the sun and earth within ourselves, the nurturing parents who will see to the fulfillment of those essentials. If we do not expect anyone to fulfill our desires, but learn instead from the plants how they satisfy their needs in the cycles of darkness and light, death and renewal, then we will return to the same primary trust that we knew as embryos inside our mothers. The plants remind us that after we have left our mother's womb we enter another protective body that will lovingly nurture us for our whole life. Therefore it is important to master all the wounds and humiliations that our desires and needs experienced from our mother.

Our mother is only a substitute for the real mother, the "Great Mother." If we start to trust our Great Mother again, who never hurt us and was always there for us, we will see the relationship with our own mothers with different eyes. Noontime is lunchtime, and we eat to satisfy one of our greatest needs. This can show us that it is necessary to discover our essential and innocent needs that will help our growth, and to separate them from the unessential and superfluous. The plants tell us: "Look, everything that we need is here. Trust and you will be cared for."

The moon and water also belong to the power of the south. The water is a symbol for the sea of emotions that are moved by the moon. In the same way that the moon is important for the growth of the plants it is important for the emotional growth of us all. Its magnetism stirs up the sea of emotions, pulls them forth, and then magnifies or calms them. We also know tides in our emotional world. The water and ocean are symbols for the inexhaustible depth and constantly moving power of emotions. But in the same way that even the deepest ocean has a bottom, even the widest river has a bed and every well has a bottom, the sea of our emotions also rests on a foundation which is the primal trust that we still knew as little children. This trust will always calm our stirred up sea of emotions, and with this characteristic truly represents the power of the plants.

The Realm of the Animals

Our Great Parents, Sun and Earth, love each other again and conceive their second child, the world of the animals, the sacred Four. This includes all swimming and crawling animals, all four-legged and winged animals and also all the mythological creatures like unicorns and dragons. In the wheel they are situated in the north. It is the opposite of the south. It represents midnight, the deepest darkness of the night. As a resting center on the extended axis of the earth, we find Polaris, around which the entire sky rotates. We can take this image as a symbol for the human plane: To be in the power of the north signifies wisdom, instinctlike action, clarity, common sense and strategies that arise out of our heart. In the same way that the entire sky rotates around the Pole Star, we can be in our center if we remember to relate everything we think and know to that abundant spiritual consciousness.

The animals teach us the power and wisdom of the north. An animal acts out of its instincts, totally sure and in harmony with the Whole. It is functioning as a link in the chain of the divine plan of creation. It knows no hesitation or careful considerations, no unnatural desires or conscience and lives in a harmonic exchange with its earthly relatives. It is aware of its mission in life and knows the necessary strategies. An animal fulfills its mission by giving all its "heart"; heart meaning, of course, its center. It acts centered, and in contrast to human beings, can never fall from its center.

This is the advantage of the animal. The least of us will be able to admit that animals have a clear picture of their mission. Our rationally trained minds will not help us much further in this respect. The rational mind is programmed for the accumulation and comfortable retrieval of information for the solution of problems. Because our mind works in this way it becomes stagnant and is unable to open itself to the abundance of real wisdom. Our science proves that it has no real answer to the questions and problems of humanity because it has lost the total view in its overspecialization.

The picture of the Pole Star should remind us that everything is related to the motionless One. Everything is oriented toward the Whole, and only this orientation gives it logic and meaning. If we think we have understood something we should not forget that we have only understood a small portion of an infinite diversity that will be closed to us if we insist on taking this partial aspect as the whole truth. Our animal relatives can help us attain our true power of mind and a healthy common sense. If we call forth and use our "animal nature," our actions may again generate in our center, and the individual will always carry the seed of the Whole. In depictions of holy men, like Jesus or the four evangelists, we will often find them accompanied by animals. This should convey to us that we can only attain sainthood or wholeness if we know the power of the animals and include them in our actions.

The medicine wheel teaches us that each of us has an animal companion as a spiritual guide—or even several—that help us fulfill our mission. Consequently, it is important that we know our animal allies so we can become one with this power that helps us act with instinctlike certainty and common sense. (How to find your animal ally will be described later, in the practical exercises.) In the same way that every species of animals has its irreplaceable position on earth, every person is called to fulfill a special function in keeping the balance of the Whole.

The Realm of Human Beings

After they had created the realm of the animals, Sun and Earth loved each other again to give birth to the realm of human beings, the sacred number Five. In the wheel, humans are positioned in the southern part and are the southern gate to the real center, symbolizing that we can experience the Divine through the power of the south. Here, our philosophy of life is supported by trust, making the world perfect as it is and giving us the feeling that everything is the way it should be. The fire of the east, the minerals of the west, the plants of the south and the animals of the north are all our relatives. We are equal to them and learn from them in the same way we can learn from each other. Humankind's specialty is language; we are the talking animal. Language creates the possibility of contact and enables us to live a communal life with others. It enables us to share our vision, and through this sharing live not just egoistically for ourselves, but in a way that allows others to participate in our lives. As the sacred Five we can meet others not only physically but spiritually by recognizing that we are all mirrors for each other.

The four directions are like a map which can help us find our center and mission. To read the map, we have been equipped with five perceptive instruments: seeing, which belongs to the power of the east; hearing, belonging to the west; tasting, belonging to the power of the south; smelling, belonging to the power of the north; and, finally, touching, which belongs in the southern part of the middle of the circle. This pentacle of material experiencing is only the first step in the unfolding possibilities of our consciousness. The powers of the four directions represent paths which help us to find our center, because it is there that the north-south and east-west axes meet. Those four main coordinates are extended by the four intermediate directions, each of which combines the characteristics of its neighbors. With their help we experience the way the Whole relates to us. Therefore the power of the intermediate directions; the sacred Six, the sacred Seven, the sacred Eight and the sacred Nine, are always viewed from the standpoint of the sacred Five.

The Realm of the Ancestors

If human beings as the sacred Five meditate on the sun, the sacred One, and unite with its power, we will experience the power of the sacred Six of the southeast. This is the unity of south and east and is synonymous with vision and trust. In this way we achieve access to the inspired spirits in the world of our ancestors who have lived their lives in spiritual awareness, trusting the sun and his light. For the sacred Five they can function as spiritual examples who can provide essence and purpose if we are able to integrate them into our plane of consciousness. It is the history of humanity. To be able to continue this history we have to understand it as our heritage, as a foundation to build our future work on. The power of the history of humanity also includes our own past lives.

What does this actually mean for us? Let us proceed on the assumption that the power of the ancestors is connected with our actual forebears from our genealogical tree. It is important to understand that we were not born at random into just any family but chose the one we wanted to live in before we were born. Everybody has chosen his or her parents and is responsible for everything that is inherited. Everything happens in its proper place in time and space. There are no coincidences and there is nothing unjust in the plan of the Great Spirit, even if that is sometimes difficult to understand. If we keep our earthly existence oriented toward its essence we will realize that our origin as spiritual beings has its source within the Great Spirit. Then it will be easier to accept everything that happens to us on earth as self-inflicted experiences which are necessary for us to unfold our hidden talents.

It is healing to remember one's heritage and to ask: Is there a golden thread in my family which I can continue to spin? Can I find a connection in my profession or work to something that my father, mother, grandparents or some other ancestor tried to realize in their lives? What is inspiring me? Which dreams were they unable to live? Which utopias remained utopias? Were there any knots in the golden thread? Can I unravel some of them?

The power of the ancestors is not only a family-specific phenomenon; it also includes people outside the family who left a legacy through spiritually fulfilled lives. Also, here is a good time to inquire about the point of contact between their lives and ours. What is it that attracts me in the life of this person? Is there a connection between their mission and mine? What has been mastered by them? In which areas can he or she be a teacher and master to me so my work, too, can become a contribution to the history of humanity?

The spirit of the ancestors can become a constant companion to us, but we will have to call and invite it to help. Only then can it enlighten our mission, and kindle our fire, transforming us into passionate beings who will dance their boldest utopias into reality.

The Realm of Dreams

If we as the sacred Five meditate on the earth, the sacred Two, and unite with its power, we will experience the power of the sacred Seven. In the medicine wheel it is positioned in the southwest, between the power of the south and the power of the west. The sacred Seven unites the trust of the south with the intuition of the west. It joins the world of the soul with the world of the body. The soul, functioning as a bridge between spirit and body, transforms the seemingly rigid housing of the body into the infinite space of the spirit by pushing the limits of fantasies, imaginations and possibilities.

We know this from our nightly dreams. There we can do anything! We can overcome gravity and matter. We can transmute into all kinds of shapes. We meet beings that we have never seen before on earth. We change our sex or become hermaphrodites. We enter into worlds that we have never seen before. We are at the scenes of action somewhere in the past. There is no limit to the creativity of our imagination.

But what are we doing with our nightly dreams? We spend about a third of our lifetime dreaming; still we are mostly inclined to separate dreaming and waking. We don't take seriously what happens at night; it is not part of reality. With this attitude toward our "nightlife" we deny an essential part of our life. The nightly dreams remind us that we have access to the invisible world already on earth.

The most important thing about dreaming is that the spiritual and emotional bodies can separate themselves from the physical body to be free to travel different regions which are inaccessible to us when we are awake. During our nightly dreams we totally live within the right cerebral hemisphere: the emotional world, the instincts, images and symbols. They can become visions that enrich our perception tremendously and constitute an inexhaustible resource if we recognize and accept them as the other side of life and reality. Dreaming frees our spirit and it soars up to its own world that it brings back to us as a dream.

The wisdom of the medicine wheel is concerned not only with the nightly dreams, but also with the Oneness of dream state and wake state. Indians consider the whole life a dream that is only complete if we understand it as a Oneness that is composed of day and night dreams. Therefore it is important to integrate the nightly dreamworld into our daydream or wake state so we can decipher and transform those symbols and images to incorporate them into our actions. The shamans encourage us to "dance your dream until it is awake" or "bring your dream to earth." That sounds nice, but how can this be accomplished? We can only understand this sentence and with it the power of the sacred Seven if we see ourselves and our earthly existence relative to the medicine wheel. In this case it means: "I" do not exist. The "I" only exists as a person in a limited body with a limited brain. But the bridge of the soul stretches above the limitations of body and brain and leads out into an unlimited world of a spirit who just thought up those limitations and gave them a material garment.

If we can manage to spiritually comprehend the material world we will feel the spiritual power influence our daily lives and change the material framework of our daydream. This makes our lives magical, because we are healed in the Oneness of day and night dreams; our cerebral hemispheres are united and not separate anymore. "To dance your dream awake" is an invitation to everyone to create meaning in life out of the abundance and perfection of both worlds, the visible and the invisible. The message of the Age of Aquarius is to link your own dream and your own life with the cosmic chain of dreams. Within the cosmic chain, the Oneness of God dreams the earth, and she dreams us; and we in our turn dream the earth, the universe and the whole of creation.

The Power of the Great Laws

When we meditate on the world of the plants as the sacred Five and unite with the power of the sacred Three, we open ourselves to the power of the sacred Eight in the northwest of the medicine wheel. The sacred Eight unites the powers of the west and north: Intuitive will and instinctlike action marry and give birth to the power of the cycles and the Great Laws.

Let us try to follow the way that leads to the sacred Eight. What do we as the sacred Five experience if we meditate on the power of the plants? Plants exhibit unshakable trust in the cycles of life. Look at the life cycle of corn: It begins and ends in the darkness of the earth. In between is the time of the sprouting seed that strives toward the light, unfolds and finally wilts and dies. However, its death already carries the seed of new life. As we can see it is not quite correct to talk of beginnings and endings. Those terms are only relative because the end becomes the beginning and the beginning is already the end. Beginning and end, living and dying, are constant change. Death is birth and birth is death. This secret is symbolized in the shape of the Eight.

When we draw an eight we realize that if we start in the center where the two circles meet we will necessarily have to return to that point to be able to move over into the second circle while changing directions. The center symbolizes the universe, nothingness, God. The sacred Eight teaches us that real transformation is possible only if it comes from the center. The shape of the eight lying on its side is the sign for infinity. Imagine this three-dimensionally and you will get a spiral movement that carries on into infinity. This shows us that no two cycles are the same; otherwise there would be no evolution. The eight contains the infinite possibilities within the finite. If we understand death, not as the end of everything, but as the end of a cycle that necessarily transforms into another cycle, we will unravel the mysteries of death and rebirth and make them our daily guides.

Like the plants, we will then be united with those infinitely finite cycles which include all life. Only through this experience can our willpower unite with our instincts and gain insight into the Great Laws that give everything its meaning and destination. Simply put, this means that we must constantly pay attention to our needs and transform them into a clear strategy so they can be satisfied harmoniously.

A deficiency will become the motor for our actions because a need always signifies a deficiency in something. If we do the necessary everyday, we will live in harmony with the Great Laws. That way we will fulfill our mission and fate like the plants that live in unison with the laws that govern their fate and surrender in trust to the rhythm of life and death. Our birth is not the beginning of our life, rather the beginning of a dream shape that condenses into a materialized body.

As spiritual beings, we are eternal and have available to us an infinite number of cycles of being which existence has in store for us. In the same way, death is not the end of our existence but merely the departure from the dreamt shape of our current physical body. To understand the wisdom of the sacred Eight, note one basic principle inscribed on a tablet of green emerald by an important Egyptian priest and initiate, Hermes Trismegistus. The tablet is lost but its contents live on to this day:

> That which is below is equal to that which is above.
> And that which is above is equal to that which is below,
> to complete the miracle of a single thing.

We can understand this law of analogy if we consider the cosmos an orderly Oneness (the Greek cosmos means "order") where all organisms, earth, sun, planets, solar systems, human beings, plants, animals and minerals are part of the great organism of the universe. Already we have seen that the body and its cells are healthy only if each cell is surrendered to the law of the highest bodily authority.

In the same way there are cosmic laws that rule Humankind. Each of us is a microcosmos that is a mirror reflection of the macrocosmos, the universe. Nothing exists outside the microcosmos that is not found within it. " . . . On earth as it is in heaven," says a famous prayer. Heaven and earth are not ruled by different laws: All outward manifestations of life are governed by the same laws. This enables us to understand the universe because we can bring it down inside of ourselves. In the temple of Delphi an inscription reminds us:

> To know thyself is to know God.

As body-soul-spirit beings we are part of the cosmic metabolism. The cosmic fabric is woven in the systematic order of its fibers. Our actual life is a cell in the cosmic body and as such it is integrated into the great cosmic cycles. The personal law of our earthly existence is our fate. It is the compass that can show us our place in the cosmic metabolism and clarify our function as "cell x" within it.

> *Again and again*
> *you will descend*
> *into the earth's transmuting breast*
> *until you've learned to read the light,*
> *to know that life and death unite*
> *and that all times are ageless.*

Until the toilsome chain of things
becomes within a peaceful ring
within yourself it rests . . .
the cosmic mind contains your will
everything in you is still—
silence
and eternity.

(Manfred Kyber)

The Power of Motion

If we as the sacred Five meditate on the world of animals, we will be united with the power of the sacred Four and thus experience the power of the sacred Nine in the northeast of the circle. The power of the sacred Nine unites the powers of the north and east. Instinctlike action and creative inspiration combine in the power of motion.

Every animal fulfills a special role or function which is in tune with the functions of all other animals. They are keeping their realms in harmony with the Whole. To understand the power of the sacred Nine we should project this image to human beings. If we want to learn from the animals we will have to ask ourselves: What is my personal role and function within the human community? This has become an important question in our times. Specialization and science, split into innumerable disciplines, allow a few people to achieve powerful positions; they claim to rule everything. We are out of context with our fellow people (there is hardly a community that functions in a supportive way—the same is true of relationships, families or professional situations), with the animals, plants, our environment, our planet and all other conscious beings in the universe. Indians would call us "orphans" because we have forgotten our "Great Mother," the earth, and our "Great Father," the sun.

How could this disruption of mind have happened? Because too many people have given away their "power" and have not taken their natural power positions that they could claim with the instinctlike certainty of an animal, if they knew about them. Too many people prefer to be ruled by someone else instead of becoming responsible and creative. Unfortunately, it is still a widespread calamity that those who know about their natural roles do not work for the benefit of their communities, but are corrupted by that power and devote all their activities to their egoistical career goals.

In the realm of the animals there is no hierarchy and the "professions" of the animals, their roles, are equal like the cells in the body where a cell in the intestines is no better or worse than a cell in the liver. It is completely unnatural to establish such measures of value. They just divert from the essential relationship of each single function to the Whole.

In the medicine wheel the northeast is also called the power of medicine. In this context, medicine means that every person's work and action will be healing and beneficial to himself or herself, others, and the whole universe. This makes every man a medicine man and every woman a medicine woman. We acknowledge that the term "medicine man" goes way beyond the meaning we usually accord it. Everybody can heal, not only doctors, priests or psychologists, if they have found their places in the Whole and are centered. Every effect which we cause has to be related to our own center because here we are dynamically connected to the Whole via our earth-sky axis. Let us look at the example of a woman who finds her medicine by becoming a baker. She has a healing effect on the Whole if she becomes aware of the correlation of all the things that are necessary to materialize the "idea" of bread. For example, she has to work with the four elements; the earth and the sun which let the wheat grow, with the water while mixing the dough, with the air while it rises, with the fire that bakes the bread—and if she puts all her love into this work, then the bread will be a healing force for her fellow people.

The power of the sacred Nine lies in integrated movements within the great cosmic cycles. We are part of this movement as soon as we discover and realize our medicine. In the Age of Aquarius we are called upon to work communally, with all people, without hierarchy or individual leaders. Each one of us as individuals should perceive our potential for power received as a vision from the power of the east, which we can actualize in our medicine with the help of healthy common sense.

The Power of the Higher Self

If we as the sacred Five meditate on the world of human beings and unite with the sacred Five, the world of the sacred Ten will open to us in the northern part of the circle. A human being who meditates on Humankind will experience the image of God, who is the power that radiates throughout the entire universe. This power is identical to our Higher Self. It is the foundation of all under-standing. When we dwell in the sacred Ten we reflect the entire medicine wheel. Every person becomes a window into the universe for the other. Each individual is like a small sun or a whirling spiral of light shining in unison with all the other suns, big or small. The Higher Self is the essence of our being, but as such it is never incarnated into the body, though it is always present. It is the aura that we find depicted in images of saints. The Higher Self belongs to the eternal spiritual realm of ideas. It is our inner source and teacher, our inner healer and the force which can lead us to perfect consciousness in the sacred Twenty, even as we live in this physical body. The Higher Self dwells in everyone. But mostly we are not able to perceive it, forcing it into the background with the power of our lower Self.

The lower Self we know very well; it loves the future, loves to create barriers; it likes to judge and condemn; it is full of expectations and is constantly comparing itself to others, is never satisfied, never silent, only sees to its advantage, and foremost only sees itself. But it is our only bridge to the Higher Self. Its function is to let us learn from all our negative or positive experiences. Sooner or later a time will come when we will no longer misunderstand all our experiences from within the bubble of our limited perception, but will expand into a higher consciousness. We can connect with higher spiritual realms only through our Higher Self. Love, for example, given without any expectation of anything in return, is a function of the Higher Self. This kind of love is like a healing force and therefore divine. Our Higher Self is the assistant of God because it is always connected to the realm of Divine Ideas. Through it we learn to be an instrument in the creative hand of God. Through it we understand that God's will becomes our will and this gives us meaning in life, healing, and shows us the way to perfection. Even though we are living within the limits of our physical body, the Higher Self lives in constant exchange with the cosmic forces and therefore provides us with the possibility of communicating with these forces.

Through total acceptance of ourselves and our duties, we will experience the lower Self more and more as a stepping-stone to the Higher Self, which encourages us to serve God out of free will. God is not a stranger outside of us; God is within us. The universe is our inner space. Shamans and other initiates constantly remind us that we can achieve true and lasting peace only if every individual finds peace within. We need to reroute the immense power of our lower Self and direct it toward the Higher Self, and use this transformed energy to meaningfully cooperate with creation. If people could meet each other on the plane of the Higher Self there would be loving communication and paradise on earth. "Every Man bears the responsibility for the place where he lives and works. He is responsible for the balance and harmony of that place with the Whole. If this kind of responsibility would be alive in everybody, peace could spread on earth." This, the answer of a Hopi grandfather to the question of whether there would be war.

In the Age of Aquarius humanity receives special assistance in fulfilling its necessary duties. These are the esoteric teachings which are the keys to the Whole. The Greek word *esoteros* means the "inner." It is the inner which dwells within the outer, the *exoteros*. As such it is always present, even though it is not always apparent.

The esoteric teachings represent the true wisdom which has always been here and will always be here. The dawn of the Age of Aquarius has kindled an increased longing for this knowledge.

The turning point of the ages has become apparent through two factors: First, we have the desire and yearning of those people who are no longer satisfied with the answers that the rational mind provides to their deepest inner questions regarding their reconnection with the universe and their religion. Thus they begin to inquire about the real wisdom. Secondly, initiates of the esoteric wisdom are much more available and more accessible than ever before. Previously, only a few chosen ones were initiated into this wisdom, but the present vision is that of a humanity where everyone becomes enlightened and wise, where everyone who asks for the required "tools" can receive them. In the tradition of the medicine wheel, the first ten powers govern our earthly existence between birth and death. But there are ten more that accompany the first ten as cosmic entities; however, we can only access these forces through the gate of our Higher Self. These cosmic beings are always present, influencing daily life through the first ten powers. Later on we will see how we can contact them through eight different ceremonies.

The Realms of the Higher Cosmic Beings

Let us try to imagine these beings from the standpoint of the Higher Self:

If our Higher Self unites with the power of the sun in the east, the sacred One, the power of the sacred Eleven will open to us, working like a higher octave or being, through the sacred One.

Eleven is the spiritual power of all the suns; it is the spirit of light and fire itself. It is the power which inspires all people (which might explain why certain social movements, inventions and so forth, occur simultaneously in different parts of the world), and not just individuals.

If our Higher Self unites with the power of the earth in the west of the circle, the sacred Two, the power of the sacred Twelve will open to us. This is the higher being which accompanies and works through the sacred Two. We can call it the spirit of all planets, the spirit of matter, the spirit of darkness or the idea of intuitive will.

If our Higher Self unites with the power of the plants to the south of the circle, the world of the sacred Thirteen opens up to us, which works as a higher being with the power of the sacred Three. We can proclaim the sacred Thirteen the spirit of all plants. The cosmic beings associated with the sacred Thirteen are all female goddesses who were the guardian angels of our mothers. We will experience their power if we free ourselves from our human mother-child relationship and recognize the earth as our real mother.

If our Higher Self unites with the power of the sacred Four to the north of the circle, the power of the animals, the sacred Fourteen will open up to us. The sacred Fourteen works alongside the sacred Four as its higher being. The cosmic beings on this plane are male gods who were helpers and counselors to our physical fathers. We can only unite with their power if we have mastered our problems with our human father and understand that he is only a substitute for the sun.

If our Higher Self unites with the power of the sacred Five, the power of human beings, the sacred Fifteen opens up to us in the eastern part of the circle. The Oneness of source and origin is experienced through the gate in the east, the power of inspiration.

Here is the spirit of humanity, the cosmic entity that works behind our species. We can call it cosmic consciousness.

If our Higher Self unites with the power of the ancestors, the sacred Six in the southeast of the circle, the world of the sacred Sixteen opens up to us, which works as the higher being of the sacred Six. The sacred Sixteen is the spirit of the ancestors. All these cosmic beings are enlightened masters and avatars like Jesus, Buddha and Mohammed, builders of bridges between heaven and earth.

If our Higher Self unites with the power of the sacred Seven, the world of dreams in the southwest of the circle, the world of the sacred Seventeen will open up to us. It speaks as a higher entity through the sacred Seven. Here are the spirits and guardians of dreams. Indians call them kachinas. In our language they are called nature spirits who give us our visions in the form of images. They are the undines, wallines and nymphs if they are water spirits. The earth spirits are gnomes, dwarfs or divas; the air spirits are trolls and sylphs, and the fire spirits are salamanders and fauns. These are powers which touch us here on earth when we are doing imaginative things.

If our Higher Self unites with the power of the sacred Eight, which is the power of the cycles in the northwest of the circle, the power of the sacred Eighteen opens up to us. The sacred Eighteen works as a higher being through the sacred Eight. It is the spirit of the Great Laws. The cosmic beings associated with the sacred Eighteen are the keepers and writers of fate, the masters of karma. They are consulted in every shamanic session to find out whether a disorder has to do with a past life or if it is karmic, and, generally, to ask for permission for the healing process. Christianity calls these powers archangels.

If our Higher Self unites with the power of the sacred Nine, the power of all motions of energy in the northeast of the circle, the power of the sacred Nineteen opens up to us. It speaks as a higher being through the power of the sacred Nine. Here we find all spirits who govern the entirety of energy motions and keep the universe in balance. They are the enlightened masters of the universe. With their spirit they impregnate the present stage of human development. Christianity calls them archaics, the primeval powers. These wise governors work only in the universe, not on earth like the enlightened of the sacred Sixteen. They are, however, accessible to us if we become aware that they have all the necessary inspiration for the preparation of our medicine, our mission. That is why they should be called on exactly for this purpose.

If our Higher Self unites with the power of the sacred Ten, the power of the Higher Self itself, the power of the sacred Twenty will open up to us. The sacred Twenty is the power of the Great Spirit, of Oneness and perfection, that pervades the sacred Five, Ten, Fifteen and Twenty. The specialty of this power is the experience of death and the knowledge that it is not an end to everything but the source of all life. As we travel our path, we must encounter death again and again, and permit growth and maturity of our consciousness to its highest level. Death is "letting go" and "giving away" in a double sense: to rid yourself of the forces of the lower self and to give yourself direction on a path. Death also is the actual destruction of life to be able to survive, for example, the killing of animals and plants for food. We may understand death as our daily companion and advisor who injects us with the power of change and motion or the alchemical elixir of life. Our earthly existence moves a little closer to death every day. If we consider this movement from the standpoint of the spirit, it will look reversed because it will move a little closer to its origin every day. In the power of the sacred Twenty, there is no longer any difference between life and death. Both are change and therefore one in spirit. In our Great-Spirit-Being, we live in the primeval state of paradise where no separation and no contradiction distinguishes us from the divine. Here we are One and can rest in the loving embrace of our primordial grandparents. The sacred Twenty is the power which makes us "holy" in the sense of whole. Everything we experience in the sacred circle will be perfected through this relationship. In the sacred Twenty, the circle comes to completion; the end becomes the beginning and the sacred Twenty merges with the sacred Zero, the center and nothingness which contains everything.

The Colors of the Medicine Wheel

Specific colors designate the four directions of the medicine wheel:

> The east bears the color yellow or gold. It is the color of the sun.
>
> The west has the color black. It is the color of the earth and darkness.
>
> The south bears the color red. It is the color of emotions, and in this case, the ones that are unbalanced and aggressive and prevent world peace. The real color of the south is green, the color of the plants. It is that of harmony and peace.
>
> The north has the colors blue or white, the color of the air.

The main coordinates of the medicine wheel represent the fourfold consciousness of human beings. They are the four paths:

> The path of the east is the gate of the spirit,
> the path of the west is the gate of the body,
> the path of the south is the gate of the emotions and
> the path of the north is the gate of the mind.

All four paths are One because they all meet in the center. They determine our center and divinity. It is important for the work with the medicine wheel that we learn to tread this fourfold path as one path. This way we can open all four gates to experience reality in its completeness.

Magical Work at Your Power Spot

In this chapter we will start our practical work. So far we have only described the theoretical form of the medicine wheel, the circle of the twenty sacred powers. The first step for anyone who wants to really use these powers is the construction of a medicine wheel. We are human—we have chosen to live on this earth in a physical form. Therefore, we need an earthly manifestation of this concept of the medicine wheel.

Creating our own sacred circle is the first magic ritual that we perform on our path to perfection. It is the basic ritual that we will use in every magical action. "Speak to the Great Spirit only from the Circle," the Indians tell us. The circle, symbol of the Whole, serves as a bond with the Divine. It is holy because it heals us, includes us in the Whole. A medicine wheel made of stones is a place dedicated to the invitation of the divine powers into our midst. It is the temple in which we commune with the Divine.

The sacred circle of stones acknowledged by our ancestors as a place of worship has become the heritage for the Age of Aquarius, a heritage dating back to the Stone Age. Because it is free of doctrines, the sacred circle alone is able to include all the places of worship of all the religions of the world. It is open to all those who seek to regain their unity with the Whole. This natural temple knows no one priest who is specially chosen to "bring the sheep back to the fold." In this temple, all build their own personal bridge joining Heaven and Earth. The temple in its form of a visible stone circle becomes a reflection of humankind's inner sanctuary. It is a tangible, visible aid that guides us to the invisible medicine wheel of our inner. Nobody can walk this path for us—no priest, no guru and no shaman master. The path requires the free will of each individual.

There are many ways of building your circle, depending on your living situation. For example, the wheel may be built out in nature, but it may also be built in an enclosed space. You also need to consider which suits your purposes better, a permanent medicine wheel or one that can be laid out and taken apart as required.

The Medicine Wheel Indoors

The simplest option is to build a medicine wheel at home that can be taken apart after use. To mark the points of the four main directions we can use stones or, better yet, objects which symbolize the particular powers of those directions: Use a candle for the east, symbolizing the power of light; a bowl filled with soil for the west, symbolizing the power of the earth; to the south put a plant for the power of the plant world and to the north put an animal (even a stuffed imitation.)

Use stones for the intermediate directions—their qualities are not so easy to represent. In the course of your work you will eventually find the right symbols. If you prefer to use stones for all the directions, you may use ones that you already have or you can go out and find new ones. Make sure that the stones have some affinity for the direction they will be used for. For example, you could use their colors as a criterion: A yellow stone would be suitable for the east, a reddish one could be used for the south, a black one for the west and a bluish or white one for the north. The stones for the main directions should be a little bigger than the ones for the intermediate directions. Another possibility is to make your own symbols. Stones could be painted or engraved with symbols, or everything could be modeled out of clay. Just choose one of the possibilities that you feel spontaneously attracted to. It is important that you remember to ask every stone that you take from nature for its permission to remove it and to leave something as a gift (we will go into this in greater detail later.)

Once you have gathered your main symbols, look for the appropriate spot in your room to build the wheel. You may already know where to put it—if you do not, then close your eyes and walk around the room. While doing this form an upside-down bowl with your left hand, functioning as an antenna to receive a signal from the right spot. The shamans call this exercise "to be called by your spot." It is an exercise in sensitizing yourself to the qualities of the different energies.

Cleansing and Dedication of the Spot

Once you have found your spot it has to be cleansed and dedicated. The best way is to use a mixture of herbs like sage, lavender or sweet grass (available from Canada), and arbor vitae (evergreen). The fumes of sage are cleansing; lavender or sweet grass smoke is used to dedicate; and smoke of arbor vitae is an energizing agent. Put the herbs into an attractive bowl, for example a shell or a carved stone. To kindle the herbs it is best to use a fan made of small feathers (traditionally a large eagle feather was used). Never blow on the herbs yourself!

Now walk clockwise around your spot three times: once to cleanse, once to dedicate and once to energize. This action brings us to another important aspect of our work with the medicine wheel: the circular movement. The medicine wheel knows two motions, clockwise and counterclockwise. Clockwise motion applies to all practical exercises that will be described in this book. It is the natural movement of humans on earth, a movement that follows the sun as seen from earth. If we follow this movement we will always be in unity with the cosmic powers; through this movement we ask for their support. Counterclockwise motion is used to conjure the cosmic powers in case of an emergency that demands direct interference of Man with the natural order. This is not without danger; just remember the Third Reich in Germany brazenly used a reversed swastika to demonstrate its power of conjuration. The power of conjuration is all too easily misused!

The Layout of the Sacred Directions

To understand shamanic action we will have to have a thorough understanding of the symbols. The layout of the medicine wheel follows the sacred way of counting: (1) the east, (2) the West, (3) the south, (4) the north, (6) the southeast, (7) the southwest, (8) the northwest, (9) the northeast. Use a compass if you are not sure of the directions. The powers of the inner part of the wheel (5), (10), (15), (20) are not being laid out right now.

Bring the symbols for the eight directions to your chosen spot. Proceed by marking the center with an object that best represents unified duality, such as the fork of a branch standing upright in a glass of water, or a stone with a double structure or twin colors. Before you lay out the object representing the center, you will have to cleanse it with smoke by holding it over the smoldering bowl of herbs and fanning it. Be concentrated on the power represented by this object and put it down to mark the center of the circle. The space within the circle should be big enough to sit comfortably inside without touching the center.

Now it is time to position the symbols for the eight directions. These you will place from the outside of the circle; you will not enter the circle until all the symbols are in place.

Start with the east, the sacred One. Take your east-object, cleanse it with smoke and place it on the place of the east. Then take the west-object associated with the sacred Two, and place it where it belongs, and so forth, (following the sacred way of counting). Proceed for all directions in the same way that you did for the center. Be aware of the significance of each direction and invoke the powers that correspond to it. We will later talk about the invocation of the powers in greater detail. Always go clockwise! When all directions are laid out pace out the circumference of the circle clockwise (!), carrying your smoke bowl and fanning it. This is to seal the wheel. The circle is now an undisturbed energy field, sealed against intrusions from the outside. It is also possible to seal it with tobacco, water or flour sprinkled around the circumference.

Before you enter the circle cleanse yourself with smoke! Start with the front of your body from your feet up to your head. Then brush downward with your feather to all sides starting at the top of your head. Finally you fan gently upward from your feet to the top of your head and a little further. The cleansing effect is much stronger if someone else is doing it, but here we assume you are working by yourself, and it is better to do it alone than not at all.

Why? What is the meaning of all this cleansing? The cleansing with smoke has a balancing effect. The sage cleanses, the lavender consecrates, and arbor vitae energizes. The fanning with the feather(s) along the body is very important; it creates an electromagnetic field that feels very comfortable to us. Our bodies always carry a field that consists of positive and negative ions. It is usually biased either negatively or positively so that we are seldom in a state of equilibrium. The ancient shamanic use of the feather can be explained by modern physics. The fanning of the body with a feather creates an electromagnetic field which is similar to the atmospheric pressure at 10,000 feet, such as on a mountaintop. Everyone who has experienced mountain air will admit that it is very soothing and energizing. This comfortable feeling is created by the equilibrium of the ions at this altitide. The herbal mixture has the same effect.

A balanced energy field around the body will positively affect all areas. It is a prerequisite for every shamanic action.

After you have cleansed yourself with smoke, walk clockwise to the south of the circle (remaining outside of it) and tap the symbolic object of the south three times with your foot. Then step over into the the circle and tap the southern point again three times with your foot. The tapping has the function of opening and closing the circle (three times stands for the sacred Three of the south). In the beginning of shamanic work it is best to use the southern gate. It gives innocence and trust, and reminds us that the one who enters is an ignorant child.

Now, be as alert as possible, and walk around inside the circle clockwise, with your eyes half closed. Your left hand should form a bowl pointing downward. Try to respond to the power! Let yourself be guided to the direction that attracts you the most; again let your left hand be the sensitive antenna that you use to receive the energy. As you practice a little and become more familiar with the process, you will be able to perceive the powers as different vibrations or prickly feelings in your hand. In all shamanic rituals the left hand is the receiver and the right hand the one that gives. This is because the right half of the body is charged positively, and is therefore able to give, and the left half is negatively charged and thus able to receive. It also has to do with the reverse reflections of our cerebral hemispheres, because the left half of the body is more oriented toward the world of the invisible and possible, whereas the right half of the body is oriented toward the world of the senses, the material and visible.

It is important to sharpen your senses if you want to track down the powers. This is always one of the first exercises that the novice of shamanism has to perform. You must sensitize your five perceptive instruments for your awareness of the material world to be brought to perfection. Therefore, try to feel the power with all your senses while walking around in the circle (but never cross the center!) until you feel a definite attraction to one of the eight directions. Go there and sit down facing the center. Meditate on the power that you feel there, open yourself to it and let it pervade you. Remember which of the eight directions has called you first because it can give you a clue about your personal place in the wheel, your power spot.

The Power Spot within the Medicine Wheel

The power spot is that particular place that each of us is bound to by fate, that we have chosen before birth as our personal source of power. If you are aware of your personal power spot you will have a lifelong companion. For example, if you have been "born into the east," you will always be attracted to the east during this ritual, always settling there first, feeling at home and close to its power, and having no difficulties opening up to it. We can safely assume that the east is your personal power spot. To be able to use this power, you will have to become acquainted with all its qualities and specialties. You will have to become allies so you can easily tap its resources if your earthly missions and duties require you to.

To continue our example this means that you have to rediscover the forces of the east, the power of light, of fire, the power of inspiration, imagination, creativity, spontaneity and the unexpected. You have to remember that the quality of this power was given to you as a special helper for this earthly existence. You have to regain awareness of it to be able to invoke it and to learn what it has to teach you. To know how to consciously turn to one's power spot is a great help.

Now, seat yourself at your spot of power, and invite it into the circle. Call it into your center, listen to its voice and receive its directions for the next step in the ritual. (If you don't happen to be in the wheel then sit down facing the appropriate direction.) The most important prerequisite to opening yourself up to the eight powers is your inner silence, your total surrender to the now, to turn off your usual flow of thoughts. Those who are familiar with meditation may use their techniques to dip into the silence. To those who don't know anything in particular about meditation we want to introduce some techniques at this point.

Different Techniques of Meditation

The "Small Death" Breathing Exercise

You can do this breathing technique while sitting or standing. If you are standing, imagine a vertical line or a tree running through your spine which will be your heaven-earth axis. If you are sitting, first make contact with the ground and concentrate on exactly the point where you are touching it with your body. Once you are sitting or standing firmly, start by taking a deep breath while counting twelve seconds; then hold for twelve seconds; breathe out for twelve seconds and hold again for twelve seconds. Repeat seven times. You will feel the growing need to gasp for air. Do not yield to that; try to stay with the breathing. In the short time span of nonbreathing you will experience a "small death." Physiologically, the neurons of your brain will be altered for a short time, and this helps to reach a different level of consciousness. This is important for every shamanic action. You will feel the change in the descent into silence and the ebbing away of your thoughts. After this breathing exercise, concentrate on the spot where you are sitting. You may perceive images and flashes—Ask all your questions aloud and listen for the answers. Do not be discouraged or disappointed if you are not successful at first. Persist! It is different for everybody.

The "Heaven and Earth" Breathing Exercise

This exercise can also be done sitting or standing. While inhaling, try to send the breath from your tailbone up to the top of your head while imagining your crown chakra opening to the heavens.

On the exhale, let the breath sink down to your point of contact with the ground and push it further in. If you are sitting, the point of contact will be your tailbone and if you are standing this point will be your feet. Now as you breathe in again, try to take with you the power of the earth and bring it up to the top of your head. On the next exhale, let the power of the heavens stream through you on its way down to earth. Continue this exercise until you actually feel the axis that connects you with heaven and earth. Then direct your attention toward your power spot.

The Singing or Speaking of a Power Word

The singing or speaking of a power word or mantra is a well-known technique. Here you will sing or speak in the rhythm of your breath. The most famous mantra is "Aum." It is the song of the earth. Take a deep breath and as you slowly exhale start singing (or speaking) "Aauumm." Then chant "Mmmaa," the primeval song of the female energy, and then sing "Rrraa," the primeval song of the male energy. If you are singing the sequence "Aauumm - Mmmaa - Rrraa," you will create a harmony on both the inside and outside of your being that calms and sensitizes you for the perception of the power.

But let us return to the circle. Before you leave the circle you will have to thank its powers, especially the one that called you. Then walk clockwise until you reach the gate of the south where you tap three times to open, step out, and tap three times to close the wheel. Put your objects away respectfully in a nice place like a leather bag or a chest. Think about your power spot; you may have already had an affinity for it before you built the wheel. Remember where you usually sit or sleep, which direction you face when you sit at the table. It is amazing how often these places correspond to your power spot. It is advisable to repeat this exercise several times to be absolutely certain you have found your power spot. Once you are sure, try to integrate this first piece of wisdom into your daily life. You can use it in situations where you need help: when you feel weak or when you cannot handle something. Just sit for a short while in the direction of your power spot and invoke this source of power which is always available to show you the next step.

A Permanent Medicine Wheel in Nature

The Great Mother Earth has chosen a special place for each of her children that is available as our personal power spot for our entire lifetime. This is a real spot on earth that waits to be discovered and established as the place of power. This is the spot where each of us should build our wheels. Then we can always return to it, physically or spiritually.

Finding the Personal Power Spot in Nature

It does not matter whether you live in town or in the country. What is important is knowing an area of complete wilderness that you like to visit and where you feel good. A park within a city is not suitable because you will be disturbed and the nature spirits have long since been driven away from such an oasis by poison, noise and pollution. You should dedicate a full day to this ritual. It is better to fast, to drink nothing, and to take no drugs whatsoever. There are several reasons for this. Most obviously, you have made this day special by your fast. You are not following your regular routine. This makes you more open to the powers of nature and you'll be easier to access. The second reason is that every shamanic ceremony demands a small personal sacrifice just to balance the taking with giving. If you suffer a little hunger or thirst during the ceremony it won't be overlooked by the spirits of nature.

Do not forget to bring a compass; your cleansing bowl with the three herbs sage, lavender and arbor vitae; a feather; tobacco; and a personal object of your choice that you can leave behind to mark the center of the wheel. Get up at sunrise. Once you are out in the wilderness, try to become meditative and calm so you can open yourself with all your awareness to the oncoming task. Use one of the aforementioned breathing techniques or do the following meditation which is specially used by shamans when they want to find their power spot.

The Energy Dance

Lie relaxed on the ground. Become aware of the points where your body touches the earth. Then breathe into your whole body by directing your consciousness into each cell. Start by consciously traveling with your inhaled breath toward the tip of your left foot. On the exhale, let that point sink into the earth. The ball of the foot follows, then your heel, your calf, your knee, your thigh, up to the left hip and finally the left part of your pelvis. Do the same with your right foot up to your right pelvis.

Then concentrate on the tip of your tailbone. Breathe strongly into it and out into the earth. Slowly travel up the spine to the cervical vertebra. Then go with your inhale into your right shoulder and breathe out into the earth. Go on to your elbow and your wrist, down to the tips of your fingers. Repeat the same procedure on your left side. Then, starting from the upper vertebra, breathe into the back of your head to the top of your skull, then down into the front of your forehead, your eyes, nose, cheeks, your mouth and chin.

This exercise should make you incredibly awake, sensitize your entire body and open all your pores to allow an exchange between inside and outside to happen. You will have a stronger perception of your whole body, and at the same time, the usual, constant chatter of the brain will be stilled. This is entirely an effect of your concentration on the breathing. Your body will be integrated into that of Mother Earth and will be easier to guide.

After you have completed this exercise, remain on the ground for a little while longer and surrender to the carrying power of the earth. Ask for guidance from the earth during your search for the power spot. Breathe in and out strongly a few times and stand up. Now imagine the top of your head suspended by an invisible thread and an elongated leg is reaching down to the earth from your tailbone. Spread your legs a little and bend your knees. Now you are standing in your natural axis that contacts the sky above and the earth below. This center is situated a hand's width below the navel and is also known as the *Hara*. Imagine your arms suspended on invisible threads and pulled upward until they are parallel to the ground. Make a gesture as if you are holding a sphere with both arms and imagine it to be the earth that you embrace.

From this point on, let yourself be guided by the energy which hovers around you. You will have tied into an energy that will carry and guide you, and make your whole body dance. Ask aloud to be guided to your spot. With your eyes half closed, do not hurry and notice everything around you: the smells, noises, animals and inner visions. Remember that your feet are walking on something that is alive and is aware of what you are doing. It will hear your request and will carry and guide you if it feels you are serious.

Finish your energy dance when you are certain that you have found your spot. Inspect it closely, maybe you already know it from your dreams. Then cleanse it with the smoke from your herbs. Start collecting the stones that you will need for the construction of your medicine wheel. When building a medicine wheel in nature it is always advisable to use stones. You will need four large ones, four medium-sized ones and many small ones to complete the circumference. You will also have to find a tree bough that branches off into two ends at the top. Remember: never take anything from nature without first asking and explaining why you need it. Always thank nature for it!

For shamans, the stones are their oldest relatives. Stones have lived on earth much longer than human beings. They have seen a lot and have been through countless changes. History and knowledge of the earth are stored within them. They are the earth's memory, shamans say, and whoever can talk to a stone and understand its language can have an insight into the immense mind of our Great Mother. Have this kind of attitude when you are looking for your stones. You can collect your stones in the order of the sacred way of counting, first the "east stone," then the "west stone," the "south stone," and so on, or you can let yourself be intuitively guided by the stones themselves. Take them with your receiving hand and ask them for which direction they are meant. Whichever method for collecting stones you choose, it is important not to just take the stone away, but to request it to serve your purpose and to explain to it why you need it. Leave a little bit of tobacco at the spot where you find each stone. Tobacco is a shamanically proven gift to the spirits of nature and is very much in demand by them. Once you have gathered the eight outer stones of direction, you will have to find four more: the ones for the sacred numbers Five, Ten, Fifteen and Twenty. These will have to be positioned close to the center inside the circle.

If your power spot happens to be around a tree, it will serve naturally as the center of your wheel. It will be your "Cosmic Tree," the streaming source between heaven and earth. If there is no tree at your spot, then look for a forked branch. Find one that catches your eye and that will be the one you call. It may already be laying on the ground or waving at you from a tree. The split branch symbolizes the bipolar primeval powers: the Mother-source and the Father-origin, and their union in Oneness.

Pick up the branch from the ground in the same way you did the stones. Tell it what you need it for and ask it for its cooperation. Then give it a little tobacco out of gratitude. If you have to break the branch from a tree, first hold it with your left hand and ask it if it is willing to sacrifice itself. If your hand feels a comfortable warmth you have a sign of agreement. You can tell a "no" by a cold feeling, and the branch will try to retract from your hand. If you feel a "yes," take your feather and sweep gently along the branch toward the trunk, and ask all the nature spirits who dwell in the branch to retreat into the trunk because you are going to break it off. This is a shamanic rule for picking plants, breaking branches or the cutting of trees.

Invocation of the Powers

Determine where the center of the circle will be, and with your compass, the eight directions. Before the actual placement of either the forked branch or the stones, however, you must call the holy powers of the center and ask them to come to your circle. Call free— really send your voice out into the universe:

"I call you, primeval Mother, you eternal nothingness who is resting in emptiness. You who contain everything, source of all life, and you primeval Father, holy creator and sacred origin. I beg you to come here into this sacred circle, into my center."

You do not have to speak these exact words or even learn them by heart, but they may be helpful in the beginning. The more intensely you work with the medicine wheel, the more intimate you will become with its powers until you find your own names for them. After you have called the powers of the center, stick the branch, with its fork up, firmly into the ground to mark the center of the circle. If you have a tree as the center, call the holy Zero, which contains all the possibilities of being, and ask it to come into your tree.

While positioning the stone of the east, turn toward the east and call aloud: "I call the power of the east; the power of the sacred One; the power of the sun; the power of fire, lightning and light; the power of inspiration, vision and enlightenment to come here to this spot, into the center of my circle." Now, dig a hole, ritually cleanse it with smoke, and put a little tobacco in it. Cleanse the east stone with smoke, place it in the hole, and bury it halfway into the ground.

This is the procedure to follow for all stones. Next is the stone of the west. Turn to the west and call aloud: "I call the power of the west; the power of the sacred Two; the power of the earth and the stones, the power of darkness, of introspection and intuition; the power of will and magic; to come here to this spot into my sacred circle."

Next is the stone of the south. Turn south and call aloud: "I call the power of the south; the power of the sacred Three; the power of the plants and of emotions; the power of innocence and trust; the power of the water and the moon; to come here into my sacred circle."

While laying out the stone of the north, turn north and call out loud: "I call the power of the north; the power of the sacred Four; the power of the animals; the power of mind, of clarity, wisdom and logic; the power of instincts; the power of the wind and the air, to come here to this spot, into my sacred circle."

When you are laying out the stone for the power of the sacred Five inside the circle to the south call out loud: "I call the power of the sacred Five; the power of the human race; of language and touch, to come here to this spot, into my sacred circle."

As you lay out the stone of the southeast, turn to the southeast and call: "I call the power of the southeast; the power of the sacred Six; the power of the ancestors; the power of previous incarnations and of history, to come here to this spot, into my sacred circle."

Next is the stone for the southwest. Turn to the southwest and call aloud: "I call on the power of the sacred Seven; the power of dreams, to come here to this spot, into my sacred circle."

Then the stone of the northwest. Turn into that direction and call: "I call the power of the northwest; the power of the holy Eight; the power of the cycles; the power of the Great Laws, to come here to this spot, into my sacred circle."

While laying out the stone of the northeast call out into that direction: "I call the power of the northeast; the sacred Nine; the power of motion; the power of medicine, to come here to this spot, into my sacred circle."

Place the stone for the sacred Ten inside the circle to the north of the center with the words: "I call the power of the sacred Ten; the power of the Higher Self, to come here to this spot, into my sacred circle."

Now, in the beginning of your medicine work, while building your circle, it is enough to communicate with the powers up to the sacred Ten; there is no need to call each of the assisting powers. As higher beings, they already accompany the powers of the eight directions and operate through them.

But, inside the circle we are still missing two stones which you will want to lay out with an invocation. Take the stone for the sacred Fifteen, and place it to the east of the center with the words: "I call the power of the sacred Fifteen; the power of human beings in the universe, to come here to this spot, into my sacred circle." And finally, place the stone that will represent the sacred Twenty to the west of the center: "I call the power of the sacred Twenty; the power of the sacred perfection; the power that brings wholeness, the Great Spirit."

To complete the circle, add small stones to connect the main directions. Seal the circle by fanning smoke around it in a clockwise direction or by spreading a ring of tobacco around it. If your circle is adjacent to a creek or a well, you can sprinkle water on your medicine wheel. Remember also to ask the water if it wants to serve your purpose. Now your stone circle is complete; it has become a holy place.

Formally enter the wheel by tapping the stone of the south three times to open it and three times to close it. As you do this, remember to start with innocence and trust. Walk the circle clockwise. Make your left hand into the antenna that we talked about before and keep your eyes half open. Keep walking until you feel the call of a definite direction. Always face the center of the circle when you sit down at the chosen place. Imagine an empty channel or pipe that runs through your body which allows that power to flow into you. From above you will receive celestial influences, and from below, the terrestrial will arise. Register everything you receive: the images, ideas, thoughts, feelings, memories and missions.

Remain sitting on this spot until you either get called to another spot or until you feel you can close the ritual. If you receive the call of another direction follow it, but always walk clockwise and never cross the center. If you feel alert and receptive enough, you can also use the other directions as stations for meditation just to feel what they are like. The more you work with the wheel, the more you will become aware of their different qualities. Everybody has the ability to develop this sensitivity, some awaken to it quickly while others take a little longer. If you want, you can make yourself a little medicine book to help you remember your experiences.

The Center of the Circle—
The Child's Fire

Before you leave the circle, bury the personal object that you brought with you in the center. This is your gift to the earth to thank her for this spot, and it is also your material connection with this place. In the language of the medicine wheel, the center of the circle is called "the child's fire." This expresses something we all know from the Bible but which is much older than the Bible: "Become again like the children, because theirs is the kingdom of God." The child's fire is the symbol of the enlightened child, of the holy, healthy child who has never experienced suffering, who only knows love and is one with the power of the great ancestors. One of the most important laws in the medicine wheel is: "Nothing may be done that will harm the children." Once you have buried your object, leave the circle through the south, by tapping it open and closed, and that is the end of the ritual. You can come back to your power spot as often as you like. If you have a garden, you can build your wheel there, as a kind of home altar.

But this doesn't exclude your having a personal power spot out in the wilderness.

The Four Shields

These shields correspond to four different powers that we all have. They are not actually part of the body; therefore, they are not material forces. We find them in the aura that surrounds human beings. The aura is the energy field that surrounds the body like an eggshell. Some people among us are able to see this lightbody. Many healers use aura reading as a support; it helps them to detect diseases and their causes. In many cases it is also possible to predict diseases because every sickness is visible in the aura before it materializes in the body.

Shamans explain to us that the aura contains four different energy centers that are seen as swirls of light. These are situated at the four sides of the body: left and right and front and back. In shamanic language these energy centers are called shields. We can imagine them as actual shields that have been presented to humankind like the shields of a warrior to help us in our survival. These four shields force us to be aware of all directions. We become the "magic warriors" who balance and direct our four shields from within and, alternatively, use them to shield ourselves from the world.

Working with the four shields does not necessarily require the ability to read auras. It is more important to understand the different qualities of the shields. Then, if we become aware of their presence in our daily lives, we will be able to read the respective qualities of the shields in the behavior of different people.

Let us first find out about the arrangement of the shields within the aura. In man and woman the shields are opposite. The arrangement also changes with adulthood. Let us first look at the arrangement of the shields from birth to beginning adulthood:

The four shields of a girl:

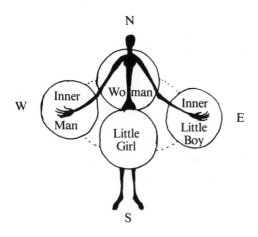

In front of her body we find the southern shield, her "little-girl-shield."

In the back of her body we find her "woman-shield," the northern shield.

On the right side her western shield is located, her "inner-man-shield."

On her left side the eastern shield is located, her "inner-little-boy-shield."

The four shields of a boy:

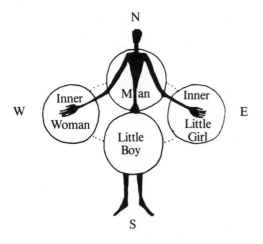

In front of his body we find his southern shield, his "little-boy-shield."

Behind his body we find his northern shield, his "man-shield."

To the right his western shield is located, his "inner-woman-shield."

To his left we find his eastern shield, his "inner-little-girl-shield."

The arrangement of these childhood shields changes with entry into adulthood:

The four shields of a woman:

We now find her northern shield, her "woman-shield," in the front of her body.

In the back we now find her southern shield, her "little-girl-shield."

Left and right remain the same.

The four shields of a man:

In front of his body we now find his northern shield, his "man-shield."

In the back we now find his southern shield, his "little-boy-shield."

Left and right remain the same.

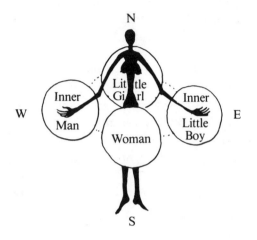

This shows the exchange of northern and southern shields in man and woman. It signifies the normal transition from childhood into maturity. We are now acting as adults, not as children anymore. The northern and the southern shields are our substantial shields. With these two we master our daily life, the visible reality. But if we are only familiar with these two shields we will miss the world of the invisible and its reservoir of possibilities.

If we connect our northern and southern shields, we create an axis called the tonal-axis in medicine language. Tonal means the ordinary reality. If we connect the other two shields, we get a second axis which is called the nagual-axis. Nagual means the extraordinary reality. The western and eastern shields are our spiritual shields, comprising those inner forces that allow us access to the invisible, spiritual world. The tonal and nagual axes meet in our centers. From this center we have the best control over our four shields and are aware of which ones we are presently using to deal with the world and which ones are best to use in which situations. In a shamanic sense, a man or woman is healthy only if he or she knows how to use the shields as equally strong forces. Only then will he or she embody the magical or Higher Self. But we will have to learn more about the power of each of the shields before we can become "a magical warrior of the shields."

The Southern Shield

The Little-Girl in a Woman
The Little-Boy in a Man

The southern shield comprises the whole history of childhood and puberty up to adulthood. It reflects all experiences that a man or woman has had up to that point. Remember that in the south of the medicine wheel, we are in contact with our soul and emotions. During our socialization, we lose the innocence and trust that we brought into the world with us as babies. We learn that love is always connected with pain. Finally, we identify with this experience and it colors all of our other experiences. Our primary trust is replaced by fear of life, a fear that haunts us even as adults.

Some of us are still fighting with our parents, trying to blame them for the pain and suffering that has been inflicted upon us. So we carry around an ever-growing bag of expectations containing our unsatisfied childish desires and await fulfillment through a motherly hand. Thus many adults still carry their southern shield in front instead of in back. They are burdened by something from the past that should have been integrated into their adult lives long ago.

Meanwhile, the power of a self-sufficient and responsible grown-up, the northern shield, is wilting away in the background. Consequently the southern shield is swelling up more and more and refuses to be equal with the other shields. People such as these are impaired because they are unbalanced. Their shields are "frozen" and their growth process has come to a halt. To become healthy and balanced again they will have to "dance awake" the other three shields. If they want to stop approaching their fellow human beings with a mixed bag of pathological expectations, they will have to become acquainted with their other personalities. The key to their balance is hidden in the nagual-axis, in the spiritual power of the eastern shield.

The Eastern Shield

The Inner-Little-Boy of a Woman
The Inner-Little-Girl of a Man

The eastern shield represents the power of a child that is healthy and untouched by education. It is given to every-body as an unchanging spiritual reservoir of power for the mastery of our life. In the unconscious, it functions as an assistant to the substantial shields of the children; without it, many of us would not have survived the traumas of childhood.

The holy (healthy) child of the eastern shield represents the power of the east. Our eastern shield provides us with excitement for the "game of life," the spontaneous and divine spark that comes as inspiration and flashlike ideas. The power of the eastern shield lets us live in the divine love of the present; there is no personal history and no fear, pain or suffering. This child is inspired by the light of the sun and lives its visions on earth. It recognizes its true parents as sun and earth and is carried by this trust to live freely. This child knows that it has chosen its physical parents for this round on earth, and respects them as representatives of the "Great Parents," but does not take them as seriously as the physical child does. The wounded child of the southern shield is always accompanied by the healing force of the eastern child. In the merger of the little girl and the little boy, the power of the child rounds out to wholeness: "Southern shield and eastern shield are dancing with one another." Now the adult can carry his or her northern shield in front.

The Northern Shield

The Female Shield of the Woman
The Male Shield of the Man

The northern shield embodies the power of a man or the force of a woman. In the north of the medicine wheel we are working with our healthy common sense that we will all have if we start using our animal nature or instincts.

As men and women, we know our role in daily life, and when we surrender to it with all our heart, like an animal, we are functioning in a positive sense because we are developing rational strategies in our mind and expressing them in our actions. The woman knows her field like the man knows his and both are working toward a smooth flow of their lives, but there is seldom a smooth flow because we are trying to do with our southern shield what should be done with our northern shield. Men and women who live in the memory of unsatisfied childish desires will not be able to unfold their northern shield to its full capacity. They will have great difficulty finding their place within the community. They are unsure about the necessary strategies to fulfill their roles or believe that they already know everything and thus only live in their memories. Obviously, this is not a very positive basis for the education of their own children. For the northern shield to reach healthy proportions, its substantial force has to interact with the spiritual power on the nagual-axis in the power of the western shield.

The Western Shield

The Power of the Inner-Man in a Woman
The Power of the Inner-Woman in a Man

To understand the power of the western shield, we have to return to the medicine wheel. The western shield is held invisibly in the right hand and represents the will that comes from the depths. If we approach our surroundings with this shield, we expose our inner, our view of the inside and the power of the imaginary and intuitive. Men will experience their inner voice, their inner space and images through the power of their inner female. Women will experience their inner vision and their intuitive side through the power of their inner male. If men and women would connect themselves with the power of their western shields they would be able to use their tonal northern shields much more effectively. To master the constantly changing demands of daily life, learn to use both northern and western shields, the nagual power.

The Tonal and Nagual Shields

The work with the four shields aims primarily at connecting the tonal and nagual shields. We saw how men or women found access to the nagual, the world of the invisible, through their opposite sex: The woman through her inner man (western shield) and her inner little boy (eastern shield), and the man through his inner woman and his inner little girl.

The shields of the nagual-axis represent impersonal powers that stem from the spiritual world. They are the original, archaic and essential human powers that connect all earthly experiences back to God. In daily life, this means consciousness and awareness have to be directed toward connection, supplementation and exchange between both worlds. It actually means for man or woman to reconcile themselves with the power of their inner opposite sex.

The separation of man and woman is only apparent, but not real, from the viewpoint of the Whole. In the tonal meeting of man and woman, both have the opportunity to find their true personal unity because the meeting of their "nagual personalities" happens simultaneously even though it remains mostly unconscious. It is important to get acquainted through the dynamics of these two "invisible persons." Many problems and pains that stem from unconscious actions between man and woman could be solved this way.

In many cases, a woman may look for her own dormant male qualities in her partner. She does not wake them up and use them within herself, but has her partner, whom she loves and adores, complement them. The same happens for the man. Such a relationship is not a meeting of two complete beings, but the meeting of two halves who try to complement each other (consider the phrase, "my better half," which reflects this kind of relationship). For men and women to meet freely as mature and integrated people, they each have to live in unison with their inner opposite sex, for woman can only touch the essential being of a man if she has integrated her inner man, and a man will only reach the true being of a woman if he has integrated his inner woman.

The Four Shields in Daily Life

When we work with the four shields, we are also working in connection with the medicine wheel. Once we are able to intimately tie the power of the four directions to the power of the four shields and use this power actively in our daily lives, they will become torches which we can hold in front of us whenever we need them.

We have all learned to respond to everything that comes to us from the outside with our tonal shields, especially the southern shield. For example, I am confronted with a new situation at work. If I react with a fear of failure and have no confidence, this means I have put my southern shield forward and am reacting like a small child who feelis stupid and unable to do anything. This reaction in the spirit of the southern shield is almost automatic; we learned to respond this way as children and have never since bothered to change. But in reality, we have four shields at our disposal. If we were aware of those, we could react in the following ways:

First, the northern shield, the woman-shield or man-shield, could get into action. Just imagine the four shields as people comprising your whole personality and helping you to become whole. If you tried to view the problem from the standpoint of the northern shield and tried to merge with that "north person," you would be able to see the problem in a much more neutral light. Your "north man" or "north woman" would maybe say: "OK, this is a new task for me, a new challenge. What do I have to do to fulfill it in clarity? Where are the connections to what I already know how to do? What can I learn from it? I will give my whole heart to it! I know I have good common sense and will use it to my advantage." This would be the right attitude in the world of the tonal.

Let us stay with our example. We could also imagine a person having the following attitude toward the situation: "Great, finally something new! I can let my imagination run wild and think of new options! It is exciting to be able to play with new things." Here, you would be speaking through your inner little boy or girl—your eastern shield.

But you still have another person inside you who wants to respond to the problem as well. This is your western shield, your inner man or inner woman: "I have a lot of energy and I can utilize it if I commit myself to the new task. It was my own doing that created this situation. The key to the solution lies within myself. I will ask my inner source of wisdom, my inner teacher, what symbol or image is connected to my new task. I will be silent, listen to its voice and receive its images and energy."

You might remember one of these "persons"; you might have even met them a few times, but you can consciously make "dates" with them, and give them an opportunity to speak in all situations. Do not let just one of them speak, but get to love all of them and ask their opinions. In your daily life remember to watch your normal shield attitude. To which shield do you give preference? Then try to see the situation from the viewpoint of the other shields. Hold them in front of you and discover how different the same situation looks. Which shield is really familiar to you, and which one feels alien?

Working with the Four Shields in the Wheel

If you are unable to solve a problem that is bothering you, it helps to take it to the medicine wheel. There you can illuminate it with the assistance of the four directions and the attitude patterns of the four shields. But if you just want to discover the potential power of the shields, it is generally helpful to enter the wheel and meditate in the four directions. This demands your own emptiness so there will be room for the power to fill you.

Try to use the previously described techniques of meditation to calm yourself on the inside. Then sit in the east and try to perceive the power of your eastern shield. Repeat this exercise in all the directions. Always ask for clarity and help. Ask what you have to do to balance all four shields. Meditate on the blockages and hindrances created by you that prevent the shields from vibrating harmoniously. Which shield creates the most difficulties for you? Think of opening some of these blockages and understand their purpose. Once you have decided to let go of a certain obstacle that is hindering the unfolding of a particular shield, you can perform a ritual where you officially discard the hindrance. Look for an object to symbolize the obstacle and bury it in the ground, or write it on a piece of paper and throw it into a fire. There are many ways or rituals we can discover.

The "let go" is a central point in working with the medicine wheel, especially for healings. The let go gives us the opportunity to discard everything that we cling to that causes sickness. It is a cleansing that only works if we really want it with all our hearts. Let go belongs to the power of the north, the power of the animals, because animals totally surrender themselves by sacrificing themselves as food for human beings.

We will have to visualize this power. In the same way the animal dies to be converted into something new, like food, or a mandolin string or a shoe, something dies in us to make room for something new. Let go is a promise to the Earth for which we are responsible. The Earth absorbs everything we let go of, and she alone transforms it into love and power. This is one of her duties.

Working with the Four Shields Out in Nature

Once you have discovered your problems with one or more shields, Mother Nature will be your best teacher in achieving balance. She provides a special work place for each of the shields.

Problems with the Southern Shield

THE LITTLE GIRL OR LITTLE BOY SHIELD

Look for a spot out in the wilderness where there is water: a river, lake, waterfall, a spring. Talk to the water; tell it of your difficulties and ask it for help. Watch the water to see how it deals with hindrances. Try to become the water and flow with it; imagine this as fully as you possibly can until you actually feel how it flows around the rocks. Completely absorb this new sensation into your body. It may sound strange at first, but actually learn from the water and trust its wisdom. If you confide in the water and surrender, it will guide you through your difficulties and show you a way to rebalance your southern shield.

Problems with the Northern Shield

THE MAN OR WOMAN SHIELD

A mountaintop which brings you closer to the Pole Star will be helpful here. During the ascent, get acquainted with your problem and lovingly accept it as a friend who has an important message for you. Ask this friend to explain everything again because you have not quite understood the message yet. Also look at your personal investment in the problem that made it worthwhile to maintain it. What was its purpose? Let yourself be called by a stone; be alert for one as you are walking along, but do not deliberately look for one. Wait until one jumps out at you. Thank it and take it with you.

Strengthen your awareness; listen to nature and what it has to say. What animals cross your path? What is their message? What plants are along your way? How does the earth feel under your feet? Feel the wind, the sun, the rain, your effort and sweat, the rhythm of your breath and your heartbeat. Speak aloud to all visible and invisible creatures and pour out your heart. Imagine you are part of nature and are meeting all your relatives.

Once you reach the top of the mountain, look at your stone to see if you can recognize an animal in it. Lie down, meditate on this animal and wait until you see it clearly in front of your eyes. Explain your problem and ask it for a solution. Or just turn to the sky above. Merge with this element through your breath. On the exhale, flow out of your body into the boundless sky, and on the inhale, return into your body. You must understand everything that you have encountered on your way up the mountain as symbols containing nature's answer to your problem. Nothing is coincidental. It is up to you to find the common thread in these symbols and to produce a whole picture that reflects the power of the northern shield and ways to rebalance it. Also become aware of your main resistance that causes your disability to handle your northern shield correctly. Ask yourself it you are truly ready to let go. If you are, take the stone and bury it in the ground. But if you feel you need more time to work with the picture that has been revealed to you, take the stone home as a reminder. Discard it only when you are sure you have solved the problem.

Problems with the Western Shield

THE INNER MAN OR INNER WOMAN

To get to know your western shield better go into a dark forest or a dark cave. On your way there, be aware of all the signs. Once you have found the right spot, lie down on the ground and become one with it. The earth-body-breathing can be helpful here. Imagine you are the earth and experience what goes on in her depths. Ask the earth out loud to show you the power of your inner man or inner woman. This is a journey into your own inner, your own darkness, and conscious exploration will shed some light there. Let a sunbeam penetrate the dark and see what it illuminates. What insights are provided by this exercise? What will you learn about the power of your inner man or inner woman? Again find out what is necessary to restore this shield. What blockages can be let go of? Once you have gained clarity, ritualize the let go by burying a symbolic object.

Problems with the Eastern Shield

THE INNER LITTLE BOY OR INNER LITTLE GIRL

Go at dawn to a flat plain or desertlike environment and find a place where you can see the sunrise. Imagine that you yourself are the sun and you are growing with the outpouring of light that makes everything alive and growing. Remember that this immense power is also inside you, represented by your eastern shield. The morning light of the sun awakens everything that has been in darkness, and everything is born anew, including us. The light of the sun enables us to greet a new day with all its possibilities for the creation of something new.

The eastern shield is solely nourished by inspiration and powered by the fire of the sun. It lives in the celebration of the unknown, the joy and happiness of pure being, and the spontaneous nature of the moment. Look into the early morning sun for a brief moment, and close your eyes. Take in its resounding image and pulsate it through your body. Meditate on the necessary steps to awaken and activate your eastern shield.

Understanding the Four Shields with the Help of Four People

Another way to become intimate with your four shields is to have them represented by four different people. The significance of the shields should be explained to them. Then determine who represents which shield. The inquirer will lie down on the ground, on his or her back. The person representing the southern shield sits at the inquirer's feet, the little girl for a woman, and the little boy for a man. The northern shield sits at the head—for a woman her female shield, and for a man his male shield. The western shield sits to the right— for the woman her inner man, and for a man his inner woman; the eastern shield sits to the left—for a man his inner little girl, and for a woman her inner little boy.

All shields face the same direction as the person lying down. If you are doing this exercise with friends, select someone of your own sex for your tonal-axis and someone of the opposite sex for your nagual-axis. The inquirer (the shieldbearer) now stretches his or her arms and takes the hands of each of the nagual shields. The northern shield puts both hands under the inquirer's head; the inquirer's feet touch the back of the southern shield.

The shieldbearer now closes his or her eyes and starts to contact these four powers, becoming aware that they are always available as allies and helpers. Now, intent on the actual problem which you were unable to solve alone and have related to the four shield people, each must try to see the problem entirely from the viewpoint of their shield and answer the shieldbearer respectively. The shieldbearer should listen carefully to what each has to say, and discover which shield he or she feels an affinity for and which one is completely foreign. Continue this exercise until the problem is completely recognized. Then you will understand how to master this difficulty in the future. This exercise can evoke an experience of Oneness which is felt as deep happiness.

As you might have noticed, we have been working with the arrangement of the shields as they are in childhood. Shamans explain that our shields have rusted in place, and we cannot alternate them into the front position. In their eyes, those who are out of touch with their four shields are sick because they are not whole. Thus, our health depends on the easy unfolding of our shields. If the shieldbearer stands up during the exercise, the northern shield can go to the front, its natural position, and the southern shield can go to the back where the northern shield was. This exchange can show the shieldbearer how the man or woman can take action in the world as the appropriate power. Again the shieldbearer has to imprint upon his or her consciousness the leap that the shields took during the ritual. This experience has to be integrated into daily life, and the shieldbearer should take frequent notice of the positions of the shields and correct them if necessary.

The Four Shields Exercise at a Tree

You can get acquainted with your shields using this ritual also. Visit a tree where you will not be disturbed. Greet it and ask it to help you dance awake your four shields. Start with your southern shield; sit down leaning against the south side of the tree, facing south. Meditate on the shield of your childhood and recall its history. When has it been wounded the most? Have these wounds healed? Is it engraved with hurts that were left behind by frustrated desires? Were its feelings hurt? Which situations led to mistrust? Was it afraid? Try and let the childhood shield speak for itself as if the child that you once were was sitting right there.

Then go to the north side of the tree and sit down there, facing north. Now work with your male or female shield on the northern tonal-axis. Again imagine your man or woman, your personality the way you present it to the world, sitting there in front of you. Listen carefully to what it has to say. Ask it how it handles its role, how it deals with daily life and if it is clear about its role within the community. What situations does it avoid? Where are its difficulties in making decisions? What doesn't it understand? Where can't it integrate things? Is there discontinuity in its actions?

Next you go to the west, and sit down there, facing west. Here you will meet your western shield which is your opposite sex within yourself. A woman will meet her inner man and a man will meet his inner woman. Most people have difficulties in this meeting, but it is only the resistance of the mind that does not want to acknowledge the inner female or the inner male. In spite of all the barriers, try to give this shield human form, and visualize it in front of you. Ask it for its peculiarities and medicine. Let it tell you about its intuitive and magical actions. Ask it where it feels accepted. Where is its center of power? What does it see when it looks inside? How does it make its will known? Does it hear the voice of its inner teacher? Which part of its being can die to allow the essential to grow?

Finish by visiting the east. Lean against the tree, facing east. Here you will meet your nagual shield, your inner child of the opposite sex. The woman will meet her inner little boy and a man will meet his inner little girl. It is the power of the "sunny" and healthy child who has always been at the side of the formidable southern tonal shield; we were just not aware of it. Ask this child of the sun for its joys. What turns it on? What stimulates its fantasy, ideas and imagination? Its spontaneity? What are its visions? Where is it creative or playful?

After you have questioned all shields, return to the north side, the place of letting go. Reflect on which shield carries the greatest ballast and of what you want to get of. Remember first what the problem's function was and what it has taught you. Only give away what you really do not want anymore. Say aloud what you want to let go of.

The out loud talking is very important because it is characteristic of human beings, the sacred Five, and is the instrument that enables us to communicate with our relatives: the stones, plants and animals. We can only receive the power of the earth if we step out of our mental plane and materialize ourselves with language. Thoughts always remain within the electromagnetic field that encloses us like a bubble. When we talk out loud or make a gesture, we prick this bubble. This is why it is important to find a ritual that can symbolically materialize the contents and intentions of your let go and transform them in the act of burning or burying. When you are completely done and ready to leave the tree, give some tobacco and words of gratitude. This ritual is done with a tree because a tree gives additional support. The power of a tree lies in its harmony and its power to connect both worlds. A tree is a living being with consciousness and is therefore able to help you.

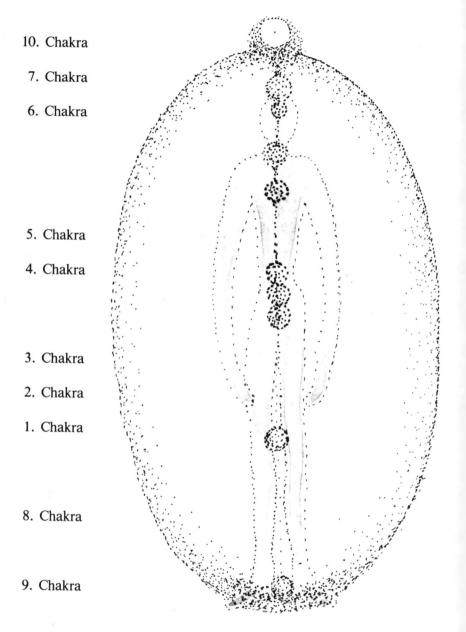

10. Chakra

7. Chakra

6. Chakra

5. Chakra

4. Chakra

3. Chakra

2. Chakra

1. Chakra

8. Chakra

9. Chakra

The Ten Chakras

The main concern of the shamanic bearers of the medicine wheel is to help us to rebuild the bridge between both worlds with the support of their wisdom. The soul is the bridge that connects the material world of the body, the tonal, with the world of the spirit, the nagual. The world of the soul consists of ten special swirls of energy, or sublime forces, that most of us know by their East Indian name, chakra. Translated it means "wheels" or "swirls of light." American Indians talk of ten different colored "lightbodies" that constitute the human lightbody. The power of eternal light shines through our lightbodies and we can participate in the cosmic energy through it. The lightbody is eternal and immortal. We can imagine these energy centers as empty vessels that each radiate a different quality of light or energy.

If we connect the ten chakras with the powers of the medicine wheel, we will be able to understand their qualities in greater detail. Our practical work will teach us to perceive them and become sensitive to their imbalances. We will be introduced to exercises that enable us to join with this subtle body for healing purposes. This must be done with the greatest care, caution and skill. Let us first examine the arrangement of the ten chakras. The first seven chakras are positioned along the spine from the tailbone up to the top of the head. Only these seven chakras are known in India and in other cultures, but the medicine wheel reveals three more that we will talk about after we have examined the first seven.

All chakras consist of sublime energy that is rooted in cosmic energy. In every person the chakras differ from their cosmic origin, but they become more perfect the more we become aware of them and the more we use them in our daily lives. It is most important to let those swirls vibrate harmoniously and feel the current that connects us with the universe and leads us to Oneness. With our tool, the medicine wheel, we can gain access to every single chakra because the cosmic powers of the sacred directions do not enter us at random, but use special gates—the chakras. Meditation on the sacred directions of the wheel is always connected with a step-by-step awakening of our energy swirls. We learn to distinguish between them, to become aware of their communication and to experience our body as a microscopic reflection of the macrocosmic unity through their flowing current of power.

The First Chakra
The Wheel of the Sun

The first chakra has its seat at the base of the spine in the tailbone and is thus called the base chakra. The medicine wheel connects it with the east, the power of the sacred One. It helps us to become aware of the power of fire and the sun and is therefore also called the Wheel of the Sun. Through the first chakra we receive the creative power of renewal that lets us share in the inexhaustible realm of ideas if we are able to surrender to it. In the vicinity of the first chakra we find our reproductive organs. In the progenitive act we experience ourselves as the creator of new life. At the same time, the merger with the opposite sex reveals to us the dissolution of all personal boundaries in the ecstasy of orgasm. The energy that we become aware of in orgasm can be experienced as a fiery current which rides upward through all the chakras producing the feeling of being pulsated by an immense power. The ability of experiencing orgasm in this way prepares us already on earth for our eternal home.

Unfortunately, orgasm is mostly experienced as a mere physical pleasure whose intoxication quickly fades and can leave behind a feeling of loneliness. But the essence of orgasm is its spiritual power which is intended to show us our affiliation with the All-Oneness. During orgasm, our ego "burns up" and we are the fire and energy of divine love. To awaken this chakra, it is important to depart from the kind of sexuality that we have learned from society and education. We have to rediscover and recreate its essence, without prejudice, and in a spirit of wholeness and health. The color of the first chakra is red. Its energy is connected to the suprarenal glands and reproductive organs. For this reason, shamanic healings always consider an illness affecting these parts of the body as related to the state of the first chakra. Healing comes from the awakening of this energy center and an understanding of its significance.

The Second Chakra
The Wheel of the Earth

The second chakra sits above the first one about a hand's width below the navel and is called Hara. Its power is of the sacred Two, that of the west, the power of the earth. If we open ourselves to the power of the earth, look inside ourselves, and penetrate into the center of our intuitive will, then our second chakra will fill up with the freed energy, and is thus able to direct our will and guide us on our way. To be united with the power of the second chakra is synonymous with being in one's center. Physically speaking it is the center of gravity, the meeting point of the axis' left shoulder/right leg and right shoulder/left leg. All martial arts like judo or karate rely on the principle of being centered in this chakra, which they also call Hara. Only through total presence of this center do they achieve mastership of their disciplines which do not primarily require physical strength, but rather conscious direction of energy.

Most people unconsciously know this power; it comes to them in moments of danger. We hear of people who perform amazing physical feats to save their lives or the life of another. If we think about these situations we intuit that these people were not the ones who acted in those moments. This immense power that suddenly works through us without giving us the chance for a clear thought is the power of magic. We act out of magic in these instances because there is no time to think about anything; the powers have the chance to intervene and help because they catch us at a moment when we are one with the power of our intuition. The color of the second chakra is orange, and the corresponding organs are the kidneys.

The Third Chakra
The Wheel of the Plants

The third chakra is a yellowish lightwheel just below the rib cage and includes the diaphragm and the navel. As seen from the spine it is situated at the pulmonary vertebra. We experience its power if we open up to the power of the plants, the sacred Three, in the south of the medicine wheel. It is the energetic conversion point of the emotions. If we are open to learn from the plants and pay attention to the trust and innocence that they exhibit in their harmonic growth, the third chakra can give us the strength we need for our well-being and emotional harmony. In the exchange with this power we feel how much attention and care is necessary for our growth process. The earth is nourishing us in the same way it nourishes the plants. The third chakra is the easiest to unbalance because our feelings are easily wounded. One bad remark and we feel sick to our stomachs! If we can manage not to wallow in negativity, but remember instead that everything that happens to us is our own responsibility, we may have understood the first lesson of this chakra. It can teach us the equilibrium between activity and passivity and the art of being while we are still becoming. Sickness in the corresponding organs—liver, intestinal tract or spleen—may occur if we have not completely awakened the power of this chakra.

The Fourth Chakra
The Wheel of the Animals

A green swirl of light is unfolded by the fourth chakra in the area of the breastbone, and it is thus called the heart chakra. As viewed from the spine it lies between the fourth and fifth dorsal vertebrae. This chakra is ruled by the power of the north, the sacred Four, the power of the animals. It gives us the clarity to recognize our missions on earth, and the mental acuity for logical thought that we need in order to achieve clear strategies for carrying them out. An animal knows its role and instinctively makes the right decisions to fulfill it. Once we are united with this power, we act calmly and do not identify with the events of life. Instead, like the animals, we devote ourselves to them with all our heart, full of love, without expectations. We would know everything if we could only transfer the animals' ability of surrender into the human realm. A truly healing medicine could be revealed if we would use letting go as a cleansing and reviving force—physically, healing in the letting go of pains and illness; mentally, in the letting go of our need for security; and spiritually in the letting go of unessential desires.

The Fifth Chakra
The Wheel of Human Beings

The fifth chakra is situated above the larynx in the area of the neck and is therefore also called throat chakra. As viewed from the spine it lies close to the seventh cervical vertebra. People who can see this chakra perceive it as blue light. We can awaken this chakra by surrendering to the power of the sacred Five, the power of human beings, in the southern part of the medicine wheel. The most essentially human characteristics are talking and touching. Real communication happens when we touch another with words that originate in our depths, words that express magic and force and are not just empty phrases. Once we prefer silence over empty words, we will be living in connection with the power of the sacred Five. Once we are connected with this power, our true voices will emerge. The entire lymphatic system—lungs, shoulders, arms, trachea, gullet, larynx, vocal cords and thyroid gland—is governed by this chakra.

The Sixth Chakra
The Wheel of the Ancestors

The sixth chakra sits between the eyes and is also called the third eye or spiritual eye. If we view this chakra in relation to the sacred Six, the power of the ancestors, we will understand the expression "wheel of the ancestors." Through this lightbody which radiates a white to violet light, we receive the power of the ancestors. The spiritual eye enables us to look into our spiritual heritage. It makes us aware of our heritage and shows us where we can pick up the lost thread. With our third eye, we can understand the spiritual connection between all beings and souls that we have been associated with in past incarnations. If we unite with this lightbody, we contribute to the endless spiritual history of Humankind and carry on its heritage. It is important to invoke the ancestors—that is what they are waiting for. It is their mission to help us after they have fulfilled their own earthly lives. They are always accessible as teachers and spiritual helpers if we request them to guide our wheel with their light. The physical organs that belong to this lightbody are the eyes, ears, sinuses, pineal gland and pituitary gland.

The Seventh Chakra
The Wheel of Dreams

The seventh chakra is on the top of the head where babies have their anterior fontanel. Its white light looks like a crown, and that is why it is also called the "crown chakra." Through this lightbody we communicate with the power of the sacred Seven, the power of the southwest, the power of the dreams, hence its name "wheel of dreams." As long as babies have their fontanels open, they live completely in their nagual, the world of instincts and dreams, the realm of imagination where they can still see the keepers of the dreams, the nymphs and sylphs, trolls and salamanders. Adults rarely remember this early dream stage of their childhood.

The medicine wheel, however, enables us to relive this age by uniting the images of the night with those of the day to experience moments of Oneness. If we open ourselves to the power of dreams in the southwest of the wheel, we will receive cosmic energy which will join conscious, subconscious and the unconscious, unifying our cerebral hemispheres. On this plane of being, the Divine will be revealed and we recognize it within ourselves. Through our dreamwheel we can experience Oneness, because this lightbody allows us to absorb the cosmic powers that intertwine us with the One. As babies, we still knew the dream that we chose for this incarnation, and we also knew our guiding nature and dream spirits. "Become like the children" admonishes the wheel! This is the only way to reconnect our lives to their divine origin. Physically, the cerebral hemispheres are connected with this chakra's energy flow. As mentioned before, the medicine wheel works with three more chakras that we will examine now.

The Eighth Chakra
The Wheel of Karma

The eighth chakra creates its energy field between the knees. Its rainbow-colored light surrounds the entire body. The American Indian shamans call this lightbody the aura of health. From its hues the shaman diagnoses various illness and is able to see whether they are determined by karma and if a healing is possible. The forces of the sacred Eight are alive and active in the eighth chakra, hence its name "wheel of karma" or "wheel of laws." Here our own laws and those of the cosmos meet. We are healthy and in harmony with our fate if we live in unison with the great heavenly cycles. Every illness is a signal that we have broken a law, but we can be healed if we find out where we transgressed and reintegrate ourselves into the cosmic cycles. If we are sick and do not live in unison with our fate and its laws, it is not only us who suffers but also the Whole. This is experienced by everyone who is trying to resist the Great Laws with autonomous and independent actions, and is therefore sick or insane, displaced as if a cancerous cell growth. If we invoke the Great Laws and ask that we be shown the laws that are relevant for our earthly life, we will have awakened the eighth light within us.

The Ninth Chakra
The Aura

The energy point of the ninth chakra is found between the feet. It encloses the whole body with its egg-shaped field of black light or energy. The four shields of human beings are located within this mantle. The powers of the northeast, the sacred Nine, the powers of motion are working through this aura. We awaken our ninth light if we "dance" with it and ask with all our devotion for the vision of our medicine. Once we have found it, we must share it for the benefit and healing of all others. Through our medicine we receive the call to become assistants of God on earth.

The Tenth Chakra
Our Higher Self

The tenth chakra's throne is about a hand's width above the head and surrounds it with a whitish-golden light, like a halo. From this light our Higher Self receives the universal life energy, the All-Consciousness. If we are in our Higher Selves, we live in the unity of the tonal and the nagual. Only through this Oneness are we magic and thus able to perceive the higher entities of the medicine wheel, the powers from the sacred Eleven to the sacred Twenty.

Awakening the Chakras

We now know where each of the chakras are located and what powers are working through them. They constitute our means to communicate with the universe. Practically, we only work with the first seven chakras, but if we become fully aware of them, the last three will be revealed to us as well.

Our breath presents the best possibility to become aware of our lightbodies. Through its rhythm we are already in exchange with the cosmic energy. Breath is the elixir of life that we pour out and reabsorb constantly. It gives us the beat and the basic steps for our "dance of life." We will become masters of our dance, if we accept the cosmos as our partner in this *paso doble* on the earthly stage: Exhale-passivity and inhale-activity are the basic steps, and in between there is silence, the all and nothing of no-breath, the moment of suspension when the dance proceeds to a new configuration.

Conscious breathing meditations can lead to the experience of "I am breathed." Cosmic breath is within us and surrounds us with the dynamic between activity and passivity, between inbreath, outbreath and no-breath. We can absorb this cosmic breath through our lightbodies as spiritual energy. It is the cosmic nectar of life that makes us immortal.

Breathing Exercises for the First Seven Chakras

If you want to do the following breathing exercises, choose a time when you can work undisturbed and without stress. Sit down on the ground to be "closer to the earth," as the Indians say. You can do these breathing exercises in your home or outdoors, by a tree or river or even in your medicine wheel where you can face the appropriate direction during each exercise.

Exercise for the First Chakra
The Wheel of the Sun

The breath of the Creator:
Breathe in slowly through your nose into your belly. Hold your breath and contract your anal sphincter as strongly as possible seven times. Let go, and breathe out through your mouth.

Exercise for the Second Chakra
The Wheel of the Earth

Female or passive breathing:
Breathe in sharply through your mouth into your chest. Hold briefly, then let breath fall into your lower belly. Breathe out firmly through your mouth.

Exercise for the Third Chakra
The Wheel of the Plants

Male or active breathing:
Breathe in sharply through your nose into your chest. Hold briefly, then let breath fall into your upper belly. Breathe out firmly through your mouth.

Exercise for the Fourth Chakra
The Wheel of the Animals

The cleansing breath:
Breathe in slowly through your nose into your belly. Hold, then lift breath up into your chest three times and let it fall back into your belly. Breathe out through your mouth.

Exercise for the Fifth Chakra
The Wheel of Man

Happy breathing:
With the muscles of your belly, suck in your breath through your mouth seven times. Push it out seven times in the same way.

Exercise for the Sixth Chakra
The Wheel of the Ancestors

The calming breath:
Put the middle finger of your right hand on your third eye, the thumb on your right nostril. Breathe slowly into your belly through your left nostril. Close it with your ring finger and hold for four seconds, then breathe out through your right nostril. Breathe in through your right nostril—send the breath down into the belly—close the right nostril, hold for four seconds, and breathe out through your left nostril.

Exercise for the Seventh Chakra
The Wheel of the Dreams

The small death breathing:
Breathe in through the nose into your belly. Hold for twelve seconds (or as long as possible), breathe out through the mouth. Hold again for twelve seconds, and breathe in through the mouth again.

All breathing exercises should be repeated eleven times in a row. In each exercise concentrate on the respective chakra and feel its power. If you want, you can meditate on each of the chakras with your eyes closed and then try to paint the picture that you saw. You can keep the order of base-chakra to crown-chakra. If you paint or draw these chakra pictures many times, it becomes especially interesting to see how the pictures change.

Besides breathing, the singing of their respective syllables and imaging of their individual colors is useful for their awakening. You can chant the matching syllable after the breathing exercise and imagine the particular light that belongs to it, or you can first do all the breathing exercises and then start with the syllables and colors. Find what suits you best!

The Notes or Songs to Awaken the Chakras

For the first chakra:
Breathe in deeply through your nose into your belly and sing aloud and full "Aaahhh" on your slow exhale.

For the second chakra:
Breathe in deeply through your nose into your belly and sing "Sol" on your exhale.

For the third chakra:
Again, breathe into your belly in the same way and sing
"Suuummm" on your exhale.

For the fourth chakra:
Breathe in the same way and sing "Eeee" on your exhale.

For the fifth chakra:
Breathe in the same way and sing "Uuuu" on your exhale.

For the sixth chakra:
Breathe in the same way and sing "Sun" on your exhale.

For the seventh chakra:
Again, breathe in the same way and sing "Auum" on your
exhale.

When you sing the notes of each chakra, meditate on the seat
and the power of the chakra. Explore its energy, how it feels and
where it wants to go. Finally, sing:

AH - U - SOL - E - SUN - SUM - AUM

This order is best to stimulate the flow of energy through the
chakras.

Color Meditation

In this color meditation you "send" the different colors of the
spectrum to their respective chakras as you breathe. For example,

for the first chakra, hold your right hand a few inches above the chakra. Let your consciousness travel to this spot and stay there on the exhale. Then imagine the color red coming from the cosmos and flowing into the chakra through your hand. Imagine in conjunction with the rhythm of your breathing.

Proceed in the same way for all the chakras. Once you have reached the seventh chakra, you can mix all the colors, giving you white light. Try to let this white light surround and cover your entire body. These exercises not only awaken your chakras but also induce a self-healing process. You can do these exercises whenever you feel out of balance, physically, mentally or spiritually.

Chakra	Color	Breath	Syllable
●	Red	Creative Breath	AH
● ●	Orange	Female Breath	SOL
● ● ●	Yellow	Male Breath	SUM
● ● ● ●	Green	Cleansing Breath	E
▬▬▬	Blue	Happy Breath	U
●⎯⎯	Purple	Calming Breath	SUN
● ●⎯⎯	White	Small Death Breath	AUM

Before we take a closer look at how to specifically balance the chakras and healing procedures in connection with the medicine wheel in general, let us discuss the subject of sickness and healing a little more.

Healing

Before the advent of medicine, priests alone held the duty of healing. The question arises, why was that so, and why was the healing profession diverted from the priesthood? The Latin word for priest is *pontifex*, meaning "bridge builder." The priests built the bridges between human beings and God, the origin. "Bridge building" was their main method of healing. Healing has always been a holy and religious act that happened to the patient, (or one being acted upon,) on deeper levels than just the physical. The "priest-healers" did not fight the symptoms of a disease; they didn't fight anything, but tried to encourage patients to accept an illness like a friend with an important message to deliver. A message that could help patients recognize their paths. The help of the priest consisted mainly in deciphering these messages in cooperation with the patient. In the priest's eyes, physical symptoms were only warning signals—it made no sense to fight them since they would just surface elsewhere if their causes were not found and treated. The priest saw that when patients *are* sick yet do not *have* an illness, what they have are symptoms, physical warnings. The basic principle, as recognized by the healing priest, was the loss of order in relationship to the Whole. The patient had gone astray in the sense that he or she was no longer in tune with fate, but had fallen from divine order and cosmic law. The wrong path is manifested physically as pains and handicaps, but the causes of these were to be found on the mental and spiritual planes.

In ancient Greece, around 1800 B.C., the Asklepiadics, the healing priests, healed people at religious rituals. One such priest was Hippocrates, who broke with the tradition of the asklepiadic art by studying diseases themselves, their purely physical activities and virulence. He devised methods of healing that had nothing more to do with religious rituals. This marked the decline of the healing priest in the western world.

Modern physicians still take the Hippocratic oath. They serve him by treating mere symptoms, and by desperately attempting to fight diseases with ever more complicated machinery and computers. But the scholars of this medicine do not want to recognize the futility of their fight—there are still sick people, and neither the scale nor scope of disease has lessened.

The symbol of the modern medical community remains the caduceus, but they have forgotten its meaning. The caduceus, with the snake that winds upward, hints at the mythological fall of Man from Paradise. Its wand symbolizes the Tree of Life in Paradise, from which the snake hangs with its head down to persuade Adam and Eve to break God's law. With this "sin" (in the sense of separation) we became conscious of our separation from the paradisiacal All-Oneness, the Divine. From then on we have suffered, trying to regain this connection. The snake pointing downward symbolizes the material and earthly, that which made Humankind sick. The upward pointing snake of the caduceus points to the heavens, to the spiritual sources and origins; it is this movement which heals us. The paradisiacal Tree of Life that became the tree of death for Adam and Eve is still, however, the Tree of Life. We only have to realize that change and motion are the basic principles of life and the eternal. The image of the snake is an expression of eternally flowing energy: birth is movement; death is movement; both convert to new forms of life, and as such they are one. The caduceus is still a meaningful symbol to wise healing priests today and one that commits those who bear it to its original meaning.

Shamanic methods of healing have kept the essence of the healing priests. The shaman understands the manifestation of a disease as a loss of equilibrium in the patient who is not living in harmony with his or her fate and the Great Laws. As Indian shamans say: "He has lost his vision," or "she has lost her dream," or "he doesn't live his medicine anymore." The shaman heals by giving new hope to the patients so they can perceive their futures again and open to the power of their visions.

But this demands that the patient take responsibility for the illness and understand the disease as a teaching. The message of the illness has to be correctly deciphered. Correctly in this context means putting his or her autonomous path in correlation with the

Whole. This is always the case in a shamanic healing session because shamans heal not by themselves, but only in connection with the cosmic powers. The patient has to accept the sickness and stop fighting it. Patient and illness have to become allies until the patient thoroughly understands this alliance and is ready to dissolve it. Furthermore, the patient has to genuinely be ready to let go of the disease, otherwise it should be kept a while longer to gain a better understanding of it.

"Man has chosen the way of sickness to become healthy and whole once more"—these are the words of a Hopi shaman. A disease is always a reminder that we should reunify our earthly existence with the cosmos.

Magical Healing with the Medicine Wheel

Shamanic or magical healing always occurs with the assistance of cosmic powers, and is therefore intimately linked to the Whole and the equilibrium between the tonal and nagual worlds. If we start using the medicine wheel as "holistic medicine," we begin to realize that we are indeed touching wholeness.

In our presentation of the sacred powers of the medicine wheel, we have been introduced to the sacred Twenty as the power of death—death meaning perfection, peace between all opposites, and as the source of life. Only the sacred Twenty becomes the sacred Zero, the sacred empty circle of divine origin that is one with the abundance of the universe and the divine creation. The sacred Twenty is Wholeness itself, the Great Spirit. If we want to heal with the medicine wheel, we must use death as an advisor because it is death that leads us back to Wholeness. Once we let our lower Selves die and enter into our Higher Selves, eternal life will flow through us even here on earth.

We now understand the ten chakras as a means of communication with the universe. To become a shaman or magician and to attain to the power of our Higher Self, each bond with the universe must be as pure and perfect as possible. The medicine wheel will help us in this by connecting each chakra with its nagual power. The following list shows which nagual power rounds out each chakra making it complete.

1st chakra - The wheel of the sun needs the sacred Nineteen, the enlightened masters of the universe, the archaics.

2nd chakra - The wheel of the earth needs the sacred Eighteen, the keepers and writers of fate.

3rd chakra - The wheel of the plants needs the sacred Seventeen, the guardians of dreams and nature spirits.

4th chakra - The wheel of the animals needs the sacred Sixteen, the enlightened, the avatars.

5th chakra - The wheel of human beings needs the sacred Fifteen, the cosmic human.

6th chakra - The wheel of the ancestors needs the sacred Fourteen, the spirit of all animals.

7th chakra - The wheel of the dreams needs the sacred Thirteen, the spirit of all plants.

8th chakra - The wheel of the body center needs the sacred Twelve, the spirit of all planets.

9th chakra - The aura needs the sacred Eleven, the spirit of all suns.

10th chakra - The Higher Self needs the sacred Ten, the Higher Self.

To understand these ten complementing pairs on more than just a theoretical level, it is recommended that you meditate on them in the medicine wheel.

The Completing of the Chakras
The Wheel of the Sun

To balance the first chakra, sit in your circle facing east. Direct your awareness to the seat of the first chakra. Do the appropriate breathing exercise or color visualization. Also, singing the syllable "AH" may be of help in contacting this chakra. Then call out loud for the help of the sacred Nineteen and ask it to assist you in balancing your first chakra. Ask what is missing for it to become whole.

With the first swirl of energy we receive our visions and inspirations—those always rely on the help of the great enlightened masters of the universe. Our ideas will only become meaningful in combination with this. Only if we let go of rigid patterns and expectations and courageously face the new and unknown will we be able to hear those voices of wisdom again and regain faith in our inspiration.

The Wheel of the Earth

To balance the second chakra, sit in the west of the medicine wheel at the place of the sacred Two. Meditate by chanting the syllable "SOL" and visualizing the color yellow. Also remember this is the chakra of the female breath. Once you have contacted this chakra, turn to the northwest, the power of the sacred Eighteen, and request it to come and help rebalance the second chakra. If this chakra is not fully unfolded, you will have difficulties with your willpower—it is a clear sign that you are not centered and do not use your intuition and introspection.

With the help of the sacred Eighteen, we will find a way to access the full power of this lightbody. Through it we can achieve knowledge of the laws which govern our fate. Through our will we can change our karma; for example, we can let go of a disease and integrate its message into our consciousness. The power of the sacred Eighteen teaches us to be responsible for ourselves. Everything that happens to us happens because we wanted and attracted it! Nobody else is responsible, not boss, not spouse, not society! We all need the living situations we created to learn and grow. If you are able to integrate this understanding into your daily life you have taken a giant step!

The Wheel of the Plants

Go to the south of your medicine wheel and meditate on your third chakra. (Get help from your male breath, the color yellow and the syllable "SUM.") Once your awareness has reached it, invoke the power of the sacred Seventeen and ask it to help you develop the power of the third energy center.

The sacred Seventeen consists of the Guardians of the Dreams and the fauns, nymphs, trolls and other spirits of nature who dwell in the various elements. These secretive beings kept us in suspense as children, led us into fairylands and magic forests because we still had the power of fantasy and imagination. Our connection to the world of the nagual was much stronger then; we believed in and talked to those beings with ease. No rational "deadbolt" was locking away this world. It was very healing for our childlike emotions.

Every child knows he or she can retreat into the world of dreams and fantasy if the world of the grown-ups becomes too threatening.

It is an instinctual survival mechanism one can relearn, not to flee from material reality, but to remind ourselves that there is another reality behind the one we know; we must remember that both realities are needed to make the Whole. We rely on the cooperation of the nature spirits—that is exactly what happens when we dwell in the realm of fantasies and dreams, thus to receive their messages.

The Wheel of the Animals

To balance your fourth chakra, sit in the north of your circle and concentrate on the seat of that chakra. The cleansing breath, visualization of the color green and singing of "E" will help to awaken this energy center. Then turn southeast and call the power of the sacred Sixteen.

Avatars are helpers who can clarify our roles within our communities. Their power teaches us total surrender to our missions, just as they themselves fulfilled their own, loving the earth and all its beings. With their eternal light they lead us back to the "path of the heart"; all we have to do is call on them and ask for their help.

Enlightened masters like Christ, Buddha and Mohammed all respected the animals as their relatives, showing us that human beings need the power of the animals to recognize our roles, and to think and act instinctively. Our thinking is insane when it is dislodged from the Whole, if it only employs selfish strategies for its own benefit and ignores the effects on the Whole. Our thinking and acting become common sense once we have achieved the ability to relate our thoughts and acts to the Whole, if we care for healing and furtherance, and if we view our own role in harmony with those of others.

The Wheel of Human Beings

Go to the southern center of the circle and concentrate on your fifth chakra. (The happy breathing, the color blue and the syllable "U" will help you here.) You will be in the power of your "wheel of human beings," giving you the ability to touch others through words. Meditate on your imperfections in this area and call on the sacred Fifteen, the power of humans in the universe. Ask what you must do to make this chakra whole. Talk to your mirror image, the spirit of humanity.

Whenever you include the Whole and incorporate your life into the cosmic history of humanity, you will get an answer from this chakra. A prerequisite for this connection is the unconditional departure from groups that are nothing but sects, with no relation to the Whole.

The Wheel of the Ancestors

Sit down in the southeast, the spot of the sacred Six, the place of the ancestors. With the help of your breath awaken your sixth chakra or third eye. (The calming breath exercise, the color violet and the syllable "SUN" will be of use here.) With our third eye we are able to see our spiritual heritage, that of our ancestors and that of our past lives. Ask yourself what is unclear, and turn to the spirit of the animals for help. The spirit of the animals talks to each person through their animal ally. Having an animal ally at your side can make life much easier; you must acknowledge your ally as a nagual power, find a way to communicate with it, and make its presence permanent. Another name for your animal ally is medicine animal. Allies help us find our medicine if we are willing to link up with them and work together with their power. The more we understand the spiritual power of our ally the clearer our mission and heritage will be.

The Wheel of Dreams

Sit in the southwest of the medicine wheel at the point of the sacred Seven. Meditate on your seventh chakra (Do the small death breathing, imagine the color white and sing "AUM.") Try to understand your life as a dream that your spirit chose before you were born. See how much you understand of this dream. Invoke the power of the sacred Thirteen, the spirit of all plants. Ask this nagual power for insight into your talents and what needs to be done to peel these out of their shells. Dream your dream of life and "dance it awake" in its completeness. Here too it is helpful to know your plant ally, thereby fulfilling one of its main functions.

The Wheel of Karma

Go to the spot of the sacred Eight in the northwest of the wheel. Try to contact your eighth chakra. At first, concentrate on the spot between your knees by sending your breath there; on the inhale, remain there and on the exhale, visualize a rainbow of colored light originating between your knees and showering over your entire body.

Then imagine that your life is nothing but a small cell in the universal body and that it must follow specific laws to function harmoniously within the cosmic metabolism. This cell is your present fate that causes you frequent pains and suffering. Ask yourself how much of this eighth swirl of light you really know. Also ask yourself which sufferings appear repeatedly and realize that it was you who chose these pains to learn from them. Invoke the power of all planets in the west, and ask them to help you complete this chakra. Through this voice, we can achieve the insight that every suffering and every imperfection can be transformed to our benefit if they become the driving force for further action. To transform weakness into strength and to encourage learning in our fellow humans is our prime duty.

The Wheel of the Aura

Seat yourself in the northeast of the medicine wheel at the location of the sacred Nine, which connects you to the power of motion, the "medicine." With great awareness pervade your ninth chakra. On your inhale, travel down between your feet and on the exhale, stretch out both arms in front of you and imagine you are holding your nagual shields, the shields of the opposite sex, in your hands. In front will be your male shield and in the back will be your little boy shield—the tonal shields. Emerge your body into a field of black energy which emanates from your feet about seven inches away from your body. This will be your aura.

Start feeling yourself inside this subtle body; find out where it starts and what its limits are. Meditate on the powers of your four shields. Try to explore their relationships. Which one is abnormally enlarged and which one is atrophied? Meditate on the difficulties that you may have with your male or female nagual power (your western and eastern shields) and which problems you avoid when relating to your childhood. With all these questions turn to the east, to the power of all suns, the sacred Eleven. They will give you directions and lead you to your medicine. The spirit of the sun shows us how to transform our personal histories into "medicine," the perfect motion of the "dancer of the four shields," as soon as we subordinate our personalities to humanity and start to be centered.

The Wheel of the Higher Self

Sit down in the northern center of the circle at the place of the sacred Ten, the location of the Higher Self. Meditate on your tenth chakra, which hovers like a halo around your head. Try to direct your breath from the place where you touch the ground upward through the spine. Imagine you are absorbing the power of the earth and that when it reaches the top of your head, it unfolds to a whitish-golden fan of light; on the outbreath it falls back into the earth. Meditate on the power of your Higher Self. Find out how familiar it feels. Does it become a gateway into the supreme reality of the nagual? Remember situations where you've let your Higher Self speak instead of your lower Self. Remember that your Higher Self is always with you as an eternal spirit and golden light. Only through the bond with this immortal power will you be immortal in spirit or in what you will leave behind as your legacy.

The Higher Self lives in constant interchange with the higher nagual powers of the medicine wheel from the sacred Eleven to the sacred Twenty. It functions like a "switchboard" through which we can communicate with these powers. The Higher Self needs the power of the sacred Ten to experience its perfection in the sacred Twenty. Call the power of the Higher Self from wherever you are sitting and ask it to assist you in the healing of the tenth chakra.

All this shows us that human beings can walk a tenfold path to Wholeness. This path is not an abstract one; it finds its concreteness in the ten chakras. Once we understand that the sublime is equal to the material it seems like something very normal. Then it is a matter of belief whether these lights exist or not; they become naturally integrated into our knowledge. This constitutes a giant leap in the direction of healing and wholeness. "HO," the Indians say, meaning "that is good."

Of course the method described above of healing the chakras is only a small step. The path to the power of the sacred Twenty or sacred Spirit is arduous and long, and everyone takes a different amount of time to complete it. But it is a path that can be discovered by everyone through persistent practice.

The Healing Power of Crystals

Since primordial times we find crystals playing a part in shamanic healing practices. Crystals have a special attribute in the realm of minerals: they can absorb and store power. They can also transmit it if consciously directed. Indian shamans call the crystal the "memory of Mother Earth" because the sun as a spiritual vision of each moment is imprinted in them as frozen light. We can release it by consciously directing our energy through them.

Healing of the Chakras with Crystals

The necessary tool is, of course, a crystal. It is important that its tip be without blemish and have no cracks. It can be any crystal: white quartz, rock crystal, smokey quartz, amethyst or citrine. It should be natural, not polished or artificially manufactured.

The next thing you will need is a pendulum. You can use any cylindrical, spherical or ringlike object that you can think of and hang it from a thread. Naturally you have to know the chakras and their position and their connection with the Twenty powers of the sacred circle.

Be aware that you are dealing with a subtle plane of human consciousness, and that the following method of chakra-balancing should not be practiced without prior knowledge and acquired skill. Only practice if you have a thorough understanding of chakras and crystals!

Chakra diagnosis is done either with a pendulum or with a method of applying pressure with your arms which will be discussed further on. Diagnosis should show how the chakras are energetically charged. You can see whether the chakra is healthy or sick, and also, if at the end of the session the chakra is diagnosed again, it will show if the medicine of the crystal was effective. Consequently, it is possible to compare the condition of the chakra before and after the healing.

Diagnosis with a Pendulum

The patient lies on his or her back on the ground. If the diagnosis is done in the medicine wheel, it has to be cleansed with smoke and the power of the four directions must be called on for help. If a medicine wheel is not available, a symbolic circle of smoke needs to be drawn—healing should always happen in a consecrated place.

To receive the vibrations of the chakra, hold the pendulum with your left hand about two inches above the chakra and watch which way it turns, whether it describes a circle or an ellipse or if it swings in straight lines. Repeat the same procedure for all seven chakras. It is important to remember the way the pendulum swings for each chakra, and probably best to draw a little diagram and immediately note the behavior of the pendulum. If the first seven chakras are in balance they will affect the last three.

Diagnosis with the Arm Pressure Method

The patient stands in front of the person doing the diagnosis. If the patient is right-handed, the left arm is extended and vice versa. The palms of the hands face outward. The examiner also stretches out his or her arm, and suddenly applies downward pressure to the patient's arm. It is very important for the examiner to remember the amount of pressure that had to be applied.

Now the examiner asks the patient to try and resist the pressure and the procedure is repeated. The examiner must get an exact feeling for the difference in pressure that had to be applied. The first time it came as a surprise to the patient, and the second time the patient was prepared; from this difference the examiner can derive a standard for the following examination of the chakras.

The patient again stands in front of the examiner and stretches out the arm he or she uses least, the palm facing outward. The examiner's left hand is put where the first chakra is and asks the patient to resist the downward pressure on the arm which is stretched forward. According to how much resisting force the patient has, the examiner can tell how much energy is present in the chakra.

Proceed in the same way for all of the first seven chakras. Take notes if you need to!

Healing Procedure

When you start working with the crystal, the patient should lie with his or her back on the ground to be closer to the earth. The crystal must be cleansed with smoke first. Then take it into your right hand—the giving—and hold its tip about two inches above the first chakra. Draw nineteen small circles and pull the crystal upward and away when you are finished. The nineteen revolutions connect the chakra to its complementary power that it needs to achieve perfection in the sacred Twenty. The second chakra needs only eighteen revolutions, and as you proceed, each higher chakra needs one revolution less. Right after your crystal work you will have to test the energy of each chakra with either the pendulum or the pressure method. The pendulum should now swing equally over each chakra, or the pressure should be the same, respectively. If difficulties with one or more chakras persist, repeat the procedure with the crystal. The chakras can be healed through the medicine of the crystal by making their energy flow harmoniously as one current. Whoever is sensitive to this treatment will experience it as a comfortable inner warmth and pulsating force.

Chakra-balancing with crystals helps immediately, but only on a delicate level at first. This means that the chakras achieve equilibrium for about one to five hours. Of course it is different for everybody depending on how sick the chakras are; still, this method can lead to a temporary state of health. Complete and permanent health will be achieved only if the patient goes through the process of chakra-meditation meticulously, the way we talked about in the last chapter. However, the rebalancing of the individual chakras is valuable because it is a real treat to have your entire spirit-soul-body touched.

This method brings about an inner equilibrium and reservoir of power that can be extremely helpful, for example, if difficult situations lie ahead. It also helps people who are in bad condition, psychologically or physically. They can again find access to their center, and strengthened by their encounter with their inner healer, gain new courage and confidence to take the next step which brings them back into motion. This treatment is also good for people recovering from a serious illness.

The Three Allies

To be able to clear our vision of the Whole, we must join again with the cycles of nature and "dream," together with our relatives from the realms of the animals, plants and minerals. Human beings were never given the mission of dominating the earth to our advantage. When the Bible says:"have dominion over every living thing that moveth upon the earth," it does not mean that human beings should become tyrants because they think they are the "crown of creation." Understand the Earth as an expression of the power of the sacred Two, and a completely different meaning will become apparent: The Earth is synonymous with the power of intuition and introspection. It leads us to our primordial will that finds expression as our center in the second chakra. To dominate the earth means nothing more than to become the master of one's inner center; to surrender to the transformation of life and death; to pervade the material with the spiritual.

In the following sections, we are concerned with our relatives: the stones, plants and animals. They do not exist just for us to thoughtlessly exploit for our purposes—they are here because we can learn from them by discovering their plane of existence and integrating this natural relationship within ourselves.

Where are our points of contact with these relatives? Following, are three shamanic practices that can help us reestablish contact with them, and also help us to find the loyal allies who will accompany us throughout life. Moreover, for its healing, the Earth needs the harmonic interchange among all beings, not only between "human being to human being, but also between human being to plant, mineral and animal," as the Indian shamans say.

The Stone Ally
The First and Oldest Human Ally

In the early Stone Age mythological story of creation, the primeval female power "Wakan" and the primeval male power "Skwan" created as their second child the Earth, the realm of minerals, sand, rocks, semiprecious stones, crystals and metals. "Brother stone" is our oldest relative. The history of evolution is engraved in him. His "eyes" witnessed the entire history of the earth from long before the arrival of human beings. The "age of the stones" has always been deeply respected by initiates and shamans, and they revere them as they would an old man who knows the secret of creation.

This attitude toward stones has nothing to do with superstition. Shamans recognize the essence of a stone when they enter into an altered state of consciousness. In such a state, they see the invisible world behind the material guise and hear the voice that talks to them and initiates them into secrets that reach far back into the beginnings of our planet.

In this magical state of consciousness we are inspired visionaries of the west, and even we could have access to this world if we would refrain from scorning it as being a fantasy or hallucination. Everybody who has seen the invisible world once will never again treat its life-forms with the lack of respect that they might have before they knew that these relatives of ours have consciousness and a specific duty within the cosmic metabolism.

The sharpening of our senses to their highest potential of awareness at any moment, and the ability to use two or three senses at the same time is a prerequisite for knitting together the tonal and nagual worlds. We, who are the uprooted and out of touch with our natural environment, have to use them as entrances to find our roots again.

What can we learn from the stones? How can we enter into an alliance with them and how can we reach a helping spirit from their world? How can this ally become an advisor to us, and why do we need an ally in the realm of stones in the first place?

To have an ally in the realm of stones is to know a helping spirit who supports the shaman in healing activities, together with several other spirits from the plant and animal realms. These allies are mediators who introduce the shamans into worlds that would otherwise remain closed to them. This meeting of the three worlds, made possible by the mediators, brings about the necessary cooperation for the shamans in their magical activities to always be able to keep the Whole in mind.

It is amazing how certain basic techniques and elements of knowledge are almost identical among those indigenous tribes where shamanism is still alive. In every shamanic tradition we find cooperation between shamans and helping spirits. And because it is our objective to learn from the shamans how to reintegrate the magical part of our consciousness into our lives, it is a step toward becoming Whole to open up our human world and integrate the other worlds within it via our helpers.

Maybe you already have a stone ally without knowing it. Think about it—try to find a point of contact with stones. Maybe you have always liked to collect stones; maybe you have a favorite stone, a pebble, or a precious or semiprecious stone that you wear as jewelry; maybe you are excited about crystals. Try to remember extraordinary encounters with stones in your dreams or in connection with diseases (kidney stones, gallbladder stones, lack of minerals, sclerosis, for example). Were you given an amulet or talisman as a present in your childhood? Spend some time thinking about this because here you will find the first clue about your stone ally.

If these questions lead you to one particular stone, keep working with that one if you already have it in your possession and not just as a memory. If you do not have it, then try to find it—if that is impossible, find one of the same family. It does not matter so much where you find it—it may be in a gem shop, in a jeweler's or simply out in the wilderness. It is more important how you find it! Your intuition should lead you to it: "This is the one, this one calls me, this one catches my eye." You also should understand that it is not only you who wants to find the stone, but it is also the stone that wants to find you. It wants to catch your attention and give you a sign to reassure you that "yes, I am the one." The stone will make you gravitate toward it once it feels your searching brain waves.

The stone's consciousness is different from ours; nevertheless, it has consciousness and the two can meet and contact each other. The stone is only able to pull you toward it if you are centered and aware when you call it (do it softly at first, but later ask it in a loud voice to reveal itself). Of course this is easier in the outdoors, but it is also possible in a shop. To further test whether it is the right stone, use the arm-pressure method; take along a friend who knows the method and ask him or her to perform the test on you. Take the stone into your right hand if you are right-handed (left hand for left-handed people), hold it in front of your second chakra, from where your intuition will give you an answer. You will be able to distinguish affirmation from denial by the amount of resistance you can exert against the pressure your friend is putting on your arm. If it is not the right one, there will be no resistance at all.

If the above have no relevance for you, go into the wilderness and search for a stone there. Do not try to do this in a park or garden. Devote a whole day to it, and do not forget to fast as a little gift for the stone. Imagine that your feet are being led to the stone, that it is not you, but the power of the earth that knows what you are looking for. You should become completely permeable, to be able to absorb the powers of nature totally. They are watching you and are ready to carry you to the right stone if you request them to do so. If this poses difficulties, meditate first to become more open. The body-earth breathing that helped you find your power spot can help you with this too. Or you can use the female breathing, the color orange and the syllable "SOL" to awaken your second chakra, your intuitive power source. In addition to all this, you can also use the energy dance to lead you to your stone.

Once you are certain that a particular stone has called you, take it into your left hand and ask it again whether it really wants to come with you. Proceed with this completely intuitively, and let your hand feel the answer. If the stone agrees to come with you, leave a little bit of tobacco behind as a gift. Now look for a spot that looks inviting to you and ask the stone for its medicine; that is, what service it can render to you. What is the power you can utilize after entering into an alliance with it? While asking this question, hold the stone above your second chakra with your left hand. Lie down on the ground and close your eyes to be more relaxed. All images that come to you are messages from the stone that you should memorize well. Then put it close to your ear to listen to what it has to say. Hold it to your nose, smell it, lick it with your tongue to taste it. Finally, feel it with your fingers with your eyes closed. Imagine your fingertips as small eyes which can see. Remember the shapes and images that you "see" in this way. Be very meticulous in this sensory investigation and integrate the results into your consciousness so you can recall these perceptions later on, even without the stone.

Then sit up, look at the stone, and turn it to all sides. Enter its history. Does it show you any shapes of animals, forms or faces? Are there any symbols or special coloring? During this meditation ask the stone again and again for the meaning of the images and signs and ask it to show its medicine. Try to combine all your findings to see if you can decipher a message or medicine hidden in the stone; look for completeness.

Before you go home, thank all the powers of nature and take the stone with you. At home, wrap it in a piece of red cloth which all shamans do to preserve its energy. The color red protects the power of such objects from disturbing influences. Before going to bed, cleanse the stone with smoke and put it under your pillow. That way it can meet you in your dreams to tell you even more about itself and its medicine.

It is best to work with the stone in this way until you are sure of its significance and the nature of your mutual alliance. It may take some time, but do not give up easily, even if after a few exercises you still have the feeling of holding a dead object. Our minds are very stubborn and do not easily accept the unfamiliar, preferring to move heaven and earth to cling to a secure and known world.

This initial step into the other world first has to develop fully in everyone to prevent that which happens to the insane, who have gone into the world of the nagual unprepared, without the keys that would enable them to unlock the doors of the tonal in order to return. You must trust that you are always watched and accompanied, even if you are not able to see or perceive the powers.

Continue to work with your stone. Maybe you will discover more possibilities for communication to unlock the world of the stone. Write down everything you experience in these dialogues and try to find the "golden thread" that runs through it all. Work with it until you know what its purpose is and how you can put it to use. During this time you might discover how to call it; it may reveal a name to you or a small melody to release its medicine and power. Repeatedly try to define the stone's medicine and become clear about the nature of your alliance with it. (For example, this stone is a male power that can help me as a woman to awaken the power of my inner male energy; this stone is teaching me to discover the talents that I need to fulfill my mission; this stone is an ally who will always answer my questions about my chakras; it is a liver stone . or otherwise significant symbol that helps me to heal my sick liver; this stone is the healing power to help me close the wounds from my childhood; this stone is my guardian who will protect me from negative influences in all situations; this stone is my vision stone for all the questions that I can't answer myself.)

There are innumerable ways to connect you and your stone. Enter your partnership with the stone in a ceremonial way. Go to your medicine wheel and sit in the place of the west, or go to the spot where you found the stone. Invoke the powers of the four directions as witnesses to your contract and read the wording of your contract out loud. As your signature, bury some of your hair and fingernails at the place of the west or the place of discovery.

In working with your stone you will find a real ally, one that will help you attain the power that will carry you beyond the boundaries of your usual self, and provide access to the "other world." Take, for example, the stone meditation: Assume you have a problem that you can't handle yourself. Perhaps you are unhappy with your line of work but you don't know what you might do instead that would be more enjoyable. You can go to your stone with this problem and ask it for advice. During this ritual it is helpful if someone beats a drum with a simple rhythm. This stimulates access to your magical powers or higher consciousness. Put the stone down in front of you, in your medicine wheel if possible. If that is not possible, cleanse a circle with smoke. Concentrate on your problem and relate it to the stone. Ask your friend to start drumming. Observe the stone from all sides, and remember exactly what you see. Only touch the stone if you want to turn it around or over; otherwise leave it in front of you.

You can move around it in a circular motion, but do not continue this ritual for more than ten minutes. Your drummer can mark the end with four strong and distinct beats on the drum. Remain sitting silently and meditate on the images which were given to you from all sides of the stone. Connect these images and try to decipher a message from them that will answer your question. Whoever trusts the stone will be amazed what a valuable advisor has been found.

By including the stone in the process of finding a solution to your problem, you are working with a power that would otherwise be difficult to discover. It is a power that dwells within the stone, but its spark will only "jump the gap" if you ask your ally for help. Only through this spiritual impulse will the power flow out of the stone to contact a specific point in your unconscious potential of power, which can be awakened and used. Had you tried to solve the problem with your rational mind, you would never have tapped your own magical source of power. The stone ally will show you a new power that is within yourself but that only becomes conscious and available through this cooperation.

This is only one example of the shape that cooperation between human and stone can take. The alliances can take on many forms and can even lead to the healing of illness. But that is up to you! The above-mentioned techniques are only meant to stimulate you to help you find your stone ally. The real joy of these introductory shamanic exercises lies in the discovery of your own ways of working that will carry a special power because you have received them as your personal visions and inspirations.

Crystals as Allies

Crystals are discussed in a separate section because they play a special part within the family of minerals. Their stored energy and transparent construction have been used from time immemorial in magical healings and ceremonies. If your ally in the world of the stones is not a crystal, it is not impossible to gain one or more allies in the realm of the crystals as well. The same rule for finding a crystal applies here—let yourself be called by the right crystal.

Make sure the crystal has a flawless tip and has not been artificially polished. Before you use it at all, it has to be cleansed and charged. Soak the crystal in salty water for three days and nights; then rinse with fresh running water. If you live by the ocean, you can use real salt water. Cleanse the crystal after each use.

Now you can charge the crystal. First it has to be charged with solar energy. For that purpose, hang it, tip up, in a tree and leave it there for one day and one night. Then bury it in the ground for two days and two nights so it can absorb the earth's energy too. It should always be stored in a red cloth.

To discover the crystal's special medicine, proceed in the same way you did for your stone. You can also utilize "crystal seeing." Hold the crystal so sunlight, moonlight or candlelight shows through. While meditating on the crystal you will get a strong feeling of drifting into the interior of the crystal. The entering of the crystal becomes a symbol for the journey into your own interior. Crystal seeing can initially be used to discover its medicine. But in addition to that you have the possibility of addressing it with your problems.

Besides balancing the chakras there are more possibilities in crystal medicine; with the help of a crystal, physical disharmonies can be balanced. Do the following exercise with a friend:

Take your crystal into your left hand and give it a message, for example, "Please make my friend tired so he can sleep." This message you only speak in your mind which must be fully concentrated on it. Then, when you think this message has "jumped over" to the crystal, hold it to your ear. If it emits a high, delicate pitch it is a sign that it has received the message and is ready to be used. You may only proceed if you have truly heard the tone, otherwise you will have to repeat the process.

Then take it into your right hand (the giving) and point its tip to the palm of your friend's left hand. Draw small circles in a clockwise manner above the palm of his hand. Your friend's eyes should be kept closed and should be completely concentrated on the perception of the crystal. Do not stretch out this exercise for more than ten minutes. Then withdraw the crystal and let your friend talk about what he has felt. If your crystal was completely infused with your mental information, the perceptions of your friend will be synonymous with the message you gave the crystal. In this example, he would have become drowsy.

After more practice, you can also use your crystal for healing purposes, for example, the treatment of headaches, stomach cramps and other ailments. Just give the right information to the crystal: "Please let her come into balance once again in her stomach (or her head," and so forth.) Once the crystal gives you affirmation, describe small clockwise movements above the troubled part of the body. If you are working on points that are also chakras, make the appropriate number of circular motions for that chakra. According to shamanic medicine all organs in the vicinity of an unbalanced chakra are also affected.

The usage of a crystal as an energy storage and energy transmitter is not a fairy tale, even though it may sound like one. The knowledge that shamans had of them has recently been discovered by physicists and brought to practical applications. Quartz crystals are used in radio and computer technology, and the ubiquitous quartz wristwatch should convince us that we are dealing with more than just superstition.

Never forget to cleanse your crystal after each use. It is enough to charge them four times a year, preferably at the four cardinal points of the sun's path across the sky: summer and winter solstice and vernal and autumnal equinox. Full moon nights are suitable as well. It is important that you never leave your crystal laying around in the open; always wrap it in a red cloth and store it in your medicine bag where it will be joined by another ally, one from the realm of the plants.

The Plant Ally
The Second Relative of Human Beings

The Stone Age story of creation goes on: The Great Father Sun and the Great Mother Earth loved each other; their first child was born, the realm of the plants: the grass, bushes and shrubs, flowers and herbs, the trees, and all magical plants like peyote, thorn-apple, various mushrooms and cacti.

In every shamanic healing session plants are present; the one being healed either lies on a bed of herbs and leaves, or is surrounded by trees, shrubs or flowers. What is the meaning of this? Plants have an inherent ability to absorb energy, especially negative energy which they can transform and reemit as positive energy. A good example of this is the absorption by plants of carbon dioxide and the subsequent giving off of oxygen. Plants even have the ability to absorb diseases if they are asked to do so.

It is no coincidence that people from around the world like to have plants in their immediate environment. They are always experienced as pleasant and harmonious, not only for the eye, but also for body and soul. Indeed, they are absorbing the negativity which we radiate into a room and emit refreshingly positive energy as a gift.

Biologists now accept that plants are living creatures with consciousness. A good deal of stimulating literature about the magical capabilities of plants has been written recently, and work being done in the Findhorn community has attracted much attention. But it is no longer enough just to listen to these stories; it is time we accept the plants as our spiritual relatives and let them know that their souls are precious to us.

For the Celts and Germans the tree was always sacred. In bygone cultures we find the tree, symbolizing the Cosmic Tree, the tree of initiation which revealed to Humankind the secrets of heaven and earth. "Hanging from the tree" or "dreaming by the tree" was one of the most important rites of initiation. Initiates experienced the tree as the stairway to heaven, and realized that trees were like their own souls, uniting body with spirit. In this Oneness, they experienced the paradisiacal state of humanity that knows no difference between creation and Creator.

Fanatic elements of Christianity caused a lot of damage by condemning this ritual as heathen nonsense which led to its extinction in European culture. But a little bit of the knowledge of the power of the trees remained in everyone's unconscious. Almost everyone liked to climb trees when they were young, built tree-houses, and even as grown-ups we like to find a tree to rest and dream by.

Plants can be medicinally used in various forms, for example, teas, essences, powders, oils and tinctures. Samuel Hahnemann (1755-1843), a "medicine man" from the western world, discovered that each person has his or her own special plant, one which becomes a helper if it is accepted as an ally and integrated into daily life. Hahnemann was the discoverer of *homoeopathy*, a method of healing which relies mainly on plants.

The basic tenent of homoeopathy is: "Let likes be treated by likes." In his experiments with plants and other organic material Hahnemann found that these substances created symptoms of disease if administered in too high a dosage. He noted these symptoms and from them developed so-called "pharmacological pictures." If a sick person came to him whose symptoms were identical with one of these pharmacological pictures, he administered in a potentized form the very substance that created this picture. The potentized form means that the plant is completely separated from its material form, revealing its pure and spiritual essence, its individuality. This essence is then transmitted as information to another material form, like alcohol or sugar, which functions as an information carrier.

Another important "medicine man" of western culture was Paracelsus, who lived 200 years before Hahnemann. He said: "What the teeth chew is naught the medicine. It is naught the body, but the force." These two men kept alive a great portion of shamanic healing alive in their work and left a legacy that is our responsibility to preserve. To fulfill this, we must find a personal ally in the family of the plants who will help us to become Whole by giving us spiritual power. It is nature's gift to us, and If we are willing to encounter the world differently, it will serve to heal us and help us become Whole. We each have a special plant that becomes our helper if we accept it as our ally and integrate it into our lives.

Finding Your Plant Ally

Let's go to work. How can you find your plant ally? Again, think about whether you have, perhaps, already encountered it. Maybe you know an herb that relieves you of a certain pain you repeatedly suffer from. Or is there a flower you prefer to beautify your home or your garden? Or are you given the same kind of flower as a present over and over? Be guided by your intuition, but do not construct something that is not there. This intuitive feeling is probably familiar to you from other situations—as an *"aha!"*—experience, or you described a dream to someone and suddenly knew: "Yes, this is the meaning." This feeling of absolute certainty was possible because understanding was already hidden within you and was merely triggered by the other.

If you are not getting any clues from these thoughts, then nature will surely help. Take a whole day and fast. Go to an area of unspoiled wilderness, not a garden or park. As soon as you are on your way, try to let the powers of nature take over: the wind, the ground under your feet (go barefooted if possible), the warmth of the sun or a rain shower, the sound of trees, the smell of the grass, of flowers, bushes, the colors. Try to use all senses, not just your eyes.

Try to hear your plant ally's call, to distinguish its fragrance from others, try to sense in the touch of a twig a sign of contact. If you feel you cannot let go of your everyday reality and get closer to nature, you can utilize the earth-body breathing, wake up your third chakra, the wheel of the plants, with the help of the male breathing, the syllable "SUM," meditating on the color yellow or dancing the energy-dance. Don't forget to call the plant aloud and ask it to reveal itself. If you do this in the power of childlike innocence and trust, the plant will come forth. Follow its beckoning, and once you have found it, talk to it as you would to a living being and ask it respectfully to let you pick it. If your plant ally is a tree, take only one of its branches or a little part of its root. Put a little tobacco at the place where you picked the plant. Lie down on the ground and hold the plant to your third chakra with your left hand. Close your

176

eyes and ask the plant to reveal its medicine to you. Pay attention and memorize every image that comes from the plant. Once the flow of images runs dry, sit up and look at your new ally.

You may be familiar with the plant and know if it is used for healing purposes. If it is unfamiliar you should find out its name and usage later on; the designation of a plant in everyday reality is always a hint, the tonal aspect of its medicine. You can also smell or taste the plant to join with it more strongly.

Healing With Your Plant Ally

Wrap the plant in a red cloth and take it home. Put it under your pillow at night and ask for a dream that will tell you more about the history of your ally, especially about how much you are interwoven with it. After the first night of dreaming with your new friend and finding out more about it, meditate on these correlations by asking: "What is it that this plant wants to show me with all its qualities and images? What can I learn from it? Which mirror does it hold in front of my being? Can it heal any of my needs or deficiencies?" Always ask the plant directly. Do not try to deceive yourself by making up the answers. Try to refine your senses to such a degree that you can really hear the plant talk.

Ask your ally where your emotions were damaged the most. Shamans indicate that hidden beneath the area where you were most hurt is your source of power, your personal medicine. This message is synonymous with the basic principle of homeopathy: "Like heals like." In whatever has wounded and humiliated us the most and caused feelings of inferiority we can also find our medicine. We have to be aware of and actively working on these issues because they disturb us like the symptoms of a persistent malady. We are the best healers for our own deepest wounds because they force us to descend into the depths of our beings if we want to close them. Carried by a strong will to survive, we can accept our wounds and transform our weaknesses into strengths, and ultimately, we can only gain. Our deepest wounds will become teachers who can show us how to turn our plight around.

A shaman will always say that permanent healing is only possible if the necessary medicine is determined in connection with the Whole. That means if we stop hiding our weaknesses and start to expose them, to make them public, we will become a mirror for others so they can learn to transform their weakness into strengths. If we stop digging around in the sore spots of others, and start to lovingly accept their weaknesses as mirrors for our own, our collective life can become the helper of the Whole. Through growing communication with our plant ally we can reintegrate primary feelings of innocence and trust into our emotional lives. We can assure the harmonic growth of this seed of trust by giving it what it needs for life as signified by its deficiencies and weak points. Bring every deficiency to your ally and ask it for help. Ask it what action is required to find your emotional equilibrium, the way a plant finds it in the sun or in the power of the earth.

If you find that your plant ally is able to cure one of your sufferings, then go out and find more of it—prepare a special medicine. According to the nature of the plant, there are several ways to do this. You can make a tea, an ointment, an oil, a powder or any combination therefrom, which can be used in different ways. It often happens that a person has more than one plant ally. In this case it is good to combine them all and make a medicine that will treat all minor and even major maladies that you may suffer from. Always carry some of it with you in a bottle or small bag that you have made for this purpose.

Another very good method is to make yourself a leather belt, sewing in a little bit of your medicine, so it will be on your third chakra when you wear it. A "power belt" like this helps you stay more centered and not become imbalanced so easily.

If you have a vegetable garden at home your ally can become a consultant to help you care for the other plants: "Give them a little more room, a little less water, more light" and so on. If you want to use other plants for healing purposes, either for yourself or others, your plant allies can help because they function as mediators between your world and the world of the plants. They can accompany you while searching for herbs and, if they are unknown to you, tell you whether or not certain plants have healing powers. The pact the shamans have with their allies goes so far as to permit shamans to ask them (even in front of the patient) which plant would be best to use and it will appear before the shaman's spiritual eye. Sometimes it is enough for the shaman to go to that particular plant, inform it about the patient's condition, and ask it to send its healing power to the patient.

Try to solidify your relationship with your ally in a ritual as well, for example, in your medicine wheel at the sacred place of the plants or at the place where you found the plant. Celebrate this alliance with all the powers; sing and dance, and give a little gift to your new friend. Remember, the more you get to know its essence, the more help you will get in the exploration of your own soul.

I must warn against the use of magical plants out of curiosity or for recreation. Their effects are often quite strong, and can cause extensive damage in subtle areas if used in ignorance. They should only be taken under the supervision of a shaman or the guidance of someone who is a master in their usage. Only if you are prepared for and knowledgeable about the cooperation with spirits of plants can their power be beneficial. It makes no sense to simply surrender thoughtlessly to the amazing flow of images and colors they can initiate. For the shaman these plants are sacred and treated with the greatest respect. Almost every shaman has an ally from this plant family, but it is a long and arduous learning process to enter into a contract with one of them. Working with the "simpler" plant allies will bring you to the point where you may feel that it is time to find a friend in the realm of the magical plants.

As mentioned above, certain illnesses or disharmonies can be passed on to the plants. You can try this with your plant ally or with a tree. Let us take an example of how to pass on a disease to your friend in the realm of plants: You are suffering from an inflamed knee. Pick some plants from the family of your ally and place them together with your original ally in a red bag for three days and nights in the medicine wheel in the place of the south. Then take the newly picked ones and separate them from your ally. Cleanse everything with smoke and invoke the powers of the sacred directions. Lie down on the ground and cover your knee with herbs. Hold your ally with your left hand above the third chakra. Send your breath deep down into the painful point in the knee, and on the exhale let the pain pass over into the plants. Be as concentrated as possible and ask the plants again and again to absorb the bad energy. Breathe seventeen times with great awareness. Then go to the north of your medicine wheel and let go of your disease with words that come from the heart. Bury the herbs you used on your knee in the west of the wheel.

Another healing method is to give your illness to a tree. Let us assume you frequently suffer from headaches. Look for a tree and ask it to absorb the pains from your head. Intuitively choose your direction as you lie on the ground with your head leaning against the trunk of the tree. On the inhale, try to send the power of the earth to the painful spot in your head and on the exhale, give the pain a push so it slips into the tree. Repeat this technique seventeen times. Finally, let go of your pains with words spoken aloud, thank the tree and leave it a little gift.

So much for my exhortations regarding the many ways of working with plants. I hope you begin this adventurous friendship and thereby make your own discoveries.

But there is yet another friend waiting for us, a friend from the realm of the animals.

The Animal Ally
The Third Relative of Human Beings

"After Sun and Earth had created the plants, they loved each other again, and gave birth to another child, the realm of the animals: the swimming, the crawling, the four-legged, the winged and all the mythological animals." This is what the story of creation from the early Stone Age tells us. The realm of the animals, as the world which directly preceded the world of human beings, has always played an important part in magic. There is no shamanism anywhere on the planet that does not include the powers of the animals. That alone should be reason enough to consider it further. For a shaman it is basically the power of this animal friend that opens the world of magic. By becoming one with this power, the shaman gains access to the legendary time when heaven and earth were still one; when human beings understood the language of the stones, plants and animals and knew no pain. Only in this Oneness, in this spiritual compendium, can humans work magically and be assistants of the cosmic metabolism.

A shaman is able to "see" the animal ally of a person, though that person may not even be aware that he or she has one! Some shamans go so far as to say that human beings could not become older than seven if not for the accompanying power of an animal. The animal ally functions as a guardian, giving us the strength to master the hurdles and dangers of our lives. During our lifetime we can have different animal allies, and it is possible to have more than one at a time.

Animals are our closest relatives, closer than plants or stones. As an allies they accompany the human being in two ways—tonal and nagual. The animal gives its tonal, or "everyday" power to us so that we can come to an understanding of the tonal role of the animal within its realm and relate it to its human tonal role. For example, you have the eagle as your friend; take a good look at the function of the eagle within the realm of the animals. What makes it stand out? What is its ecological function? The unique characteristic of the eagle is its sharp vision and its view of everything from enormous heights. It is a predator, and this means that it keeps certain areas in balance which is vital for the interplay of the different worlds of human beings, plants and animals.

Proceed in this fashion, find out about the tonal functions of the eagle, which can point to your function and mission within the Whole. An animal knows its destiny and fulfills it with instinctive clarity. This is its tonal power, something you can understand with the help of your animal ally.

The nagual aspect of the animal ally differs individually—the eagle, for example, will open the gate to the nagual, the extraordinary reality, differently for everyone. It is our task to find out what this specific gate is so we can clearly define our alliance with this animal. This spiritual power allows us to penetrate a realm we could call our "other Self" or "magical Self." If we are willing to unite with this power we will merge with our nagual essence. Therefore it is a custom among the Indians to bear the name of their animal ally along with their own name. It is the "medicine name" that one is called to be reminded of his or her mission, and also to make others aware of this mission.

You can find your animal ally in different ways. But there is a specific shamanic ceremony designed to find your friend; I would like to present this ritual here. If you want to take part in this journey, you should do so only under the guidance of an experienced initiate. We will need drums and rattles to create a certain rhythm.

Before I discuss the ritual itself, I would like to mention the meaning and power of the drum and rattle that are essential to every ceremony and ritual. As we have learned, each shamanic action requires an altered state of consciousness which we have called higher or magical. In this state the shaman sees, sees with the spiritual eye, becoming a visionary, inspired by the divine. Only in this state of consciousness do we step behind the material curtain of reality where everything that was invisible becomes visible. This state is a prerequisite for magical action; it makes contact with the beings of the invisible world possible.

The monotonous rhythm of drum and rattle helps to attain this shamanic state of consciousness. This has been confirmed by recent brain research: The sound of drums and rattles causes changes in the central nervous systems of human beings. Experiments showed that drum frequencies of four to seven hertz cause trancelike states. Because drum beats are of a low frequency, they can carry more energy to the brain than a high frequency sound source. This is because, " . . . the receptors for low frequencies in the ear are more resistant than the receptors for high frequencies and can withstand stronger sound waves before feeling pain." (Andrew Neher, "A Physical Explanation of Unusual Behavior," in: *Ceremonies Involving Drums*, p. 152) Shaking the rattle assists this process and the effect is heightened.

Of course there are other means available in shamanic tradition to alter your state of consciousness, such as the use of "magical plants." But only resort to these under the guidance of a master who is able to initiate you into their uses. For our purposes, a drum is more than enough to carry us out of our everyday reality.

A Journey into the Realm of the Animals

Perform this ritual in the dark, either in a completely darkened room at night or under the sky on a moonless night. If you are working in the open, you should take care not to disturb anyone with the sound of the drum and rattle.

First of all, the participants of the ritual are cleansed with smoke. The leader invokes the sacred powers, especially the power of the north, the power of the animals, and requests their support for those participants searching for their animal allies. All participants lie on the ground, their heads facing north. Drum and rattle players sit to the south. The leader now advises those lying down to close their eyes and visualize the entrance to a cave that they have seen in real life. It may also be a hole in the ground, a spring or an opening in a tree. The most important thing is to really know the place so that there can be a vivid picture of it before your spiritual eye.

Once all participants have found this entrance, the drum starts; it accompanies the entire session with a common timing, the beat of the north. In the beginning of the journey, only the ONE beat is played: ONE- (two-three-four), ONE- (two-three-four). This monotonous rhythm can be played quite hard when you start diving into the opening that you see in front of you. Keep your eyes closed the whole time!

A tunnel will lead you deeper and deeper into the earth. Be aware of everything that you can smell, hear, see, feel and sometimes even taste. Once in a while you may get the feeling of being stuck— just keep going in spite of all the hindrances. Use your hands like shovels. If you have difficulty getting through the opening at all, or immediately find yourself stuck in the tunnel, try the process again from the beginning, as often as necessary.

After about three minutes, the drum and rattle hit the last beat, pause for a whole measure, and then change over to a faster rhythm, in which every beat is played, (ONE-two-three-four), with the first beat still accentuated. Try to reach the end of the tunnel, which you will probably see as a bright circle of light coming toward you, getting bigger, until finally you are in front of it. Leave the tunnel through this opening, and you will find yourself in a landscape that you should inspect closely. If there were no animals in the tunnel so far, you will see them now. For the most part, these will be animals as you know them, but there may be some mythological creatures among them such as dragons, unicorns or beings that are half human, half animal. You should pay great attention to the way the animals are reacting to you, the traveler. Do they perceive your presence? Do they come running toward you? Are they showing you something or saying anything?

If one of the animals behaves in a distinctive way, or shows itself four times (usually showing all four sides of its body), it is a clear sign that this is your ally who is glad not to have to wait any longer for you. You must ask this animal if it is willing to accompany you into your world, and stay with you as your ally and helper.

The reaction of this animal will be unmistakable. If it is willing to come with you, carefully take it into your hands (this gesture is not just imagined but actually done with your hands) and hold it over your chest on your fourth chakra, the wheel of the animals.

After about five minutes the drum returns to its initial rhythm, thus giving the sign for departure. Everyone returns to the opening of the tunnel and climbs back out, with their animal on their chests. A strong beat marks the end of the drum playing and rattle shaking. The participants remain lying down for awhile feeling the power of their animal. Those who have found their animals sit upright, still holding their animals on their chests, still concentrating on its power. The leader then visits all those who have returned with an animal. The "finder" describes the animal so the leader can get a clear picture of what it looks like. With this picture in mind, the leader bends over to reach the seventh chakra, the fontanel, and blows the power of the animal into it. The leader then uses a rattle to draw four circles which closes the spot. Now the power of the animal is firmly anchored in the etheric body of its owner.

After this the animal must be "danced." Drum and rattle play a fast beat in 4/4 time. Try to let the animal dance within you and be just a vehicle for this newly found energy. Surrender to any urge you might feel: crawl, curl, roll and jump or flap your wings. Voice any sounds the animal might want to make. It is advisable to keep your eyes half closed to feel this power in a more concentrated way. The purpose of the animal dance is to get to know the animal better and to merge with it more and more.

Regardless of people's cultural backgrounds, unity with their animal ally provides a method of leaving their everyday reality to explore an extraordinary world under the guidance of a friend, who helps them bring some of it back into their daily life. The ally creates a bridge between normal and magical consciousness. Knowing how to cooperate with the friend and keep in touch with its power opens up a source of health and protection for humans; but if we do not nourish this relationship, the power will quickly dwindle.

The kind of animal that we have as an ally is very significant for the recognition of our missions and medicines. Let us remember what we can learn from the animals: Every animal knows its assigned role; a bird has a different ecological function than a bear or a mouse. The animals teach us total surrender to our function by the consistency with which they fulfill their roles, the instinct that they show in their actions, and the interplay of their roles help maintain the ecological equilibrium. The world of the animals and their systems of roles is a symbol that demonstrates natural order for human beings and their communities. If an animal were to go insane and leave the inner harmony and law of its role, the entire animal community would suffer from the disturbance of their equilibrium.

For those who were not successful in their first journey, it is advisable to repeat it, but not more than four times a day. You need not be worried—your animal will reveal itself when your search is intense enough. A common difficulty lies in the inadequate visualization of the entrance to the earth; it has to be seen as clearly as if you were actually standing right there. It is helpful to go look again at the original place in nature to help you visualize it better. The slide down into the interior of the earth can pose another difficulty; you may get stuck right under the surface and may not reach the deeper realm of the power animals. In this case it is helpful to dive deeply right on the first beat of the drum and make swimming movements with your arms to assist you. The greatest hurdle is presented by the restlessness of your thoughts; if you try to concentrate on the images you encounter and if you let yourself be carried by the beat of the drum, nothing can prevent you from entering that world. Everything can be mastered if you really want to.

What are the prospects for further cooperation between you and the "power animal" or animal ally? First, try to reexperience the various stages of the journey. Remember whether your animal had said or shown something to you. These clues are very important, because they contain the first steps toward your mutual cooperation. Now try to find a connection with the animal in previous events or dreams. Then start to connect the role of the animal with your world in the way we have already described. In case you don't know enough about your friend, read books that tell you more about it. If you can, go and watch this animal in its natural habitat and study its behavior.

The next step is to find a related "power object" which is charged with the energy of the animal and belongs in your medicine bag along with the other accessories. If your ally is a bird, the best power object will be a feather; if it is a tiger or wild cat, it can be a claw or tooth; if it is a horse, use hair from its tail or a hoof. Any part of the animal will work as long as it is related to your personal friend. It often happens that you already have the right object without quite knowing why. Or it happens that you naturally stumble upon the right object after you have found your ally, it could be in the wilderness or even in a shop. It will not be a coincidence but in accordance with natural laws.

The workings of the laws of synchronicity and resonance are understood by the shaman as signs that the nagual powers are employed and flowing. We know the law of resonance from physics. The Latin *resonare* means "to vibrate"; a tuning fork will resonate only if it is stimulated by its own frequency and will not respond to other notes. This law also holds true for human beings: Only that which has been awakened by our own "frequency" will resonate and respond to stimulations from the outside. Now, suddenly, we can see the connection between the dusty tiger claw on the shelf and our power animal which turns out to be a tiger. You could not understand this connection before because it did not belong to your personal vibration, your own frequency.

The law of synchronicity works in a similar way: Shortly after you have found your ally, someone may give you a part of that animal—a feather, a belt made from its skin, and so forth. This is an effect of your own power and affinity that is connecting you with related vibrations in your environment. Pay attention to evidence of adherence to these laws in your ritual actions; they are positive signs and echoes.

The first thing to do with your power object is to cleanse it; either in salty water, in a spring or river, or even in the ocean. Hang furs and skins in a tree for four days and four nights. Before and after you use the object, cleanse it with smoke. Wrap it in a red cloth after use and put it in your medicine bag along with everything else. The bag you can make yourself and ornament with symbols. It is important to safely store your medicine helpers.

The purpose of a power object is to become a bearer of power, charged with the power it symbolizes. Therefore, the symbol of your ally should be charged with its power. This enables you to tap directly into its network of energy and transmit it to others, for example in healing sessions. The more intimate you become with the power of your friend, the more power becomes available to charge your symbol. Put it under your pillow at night and meditate on your ally, or dance with it while wearing the object. Work with your nightly dream images: Which power is revealed within them? Are there any connections to your animal? Dreams in which you actually see your ally are a special gift from the guardians of the dreams. This does not happen very often and should be integrated into your daily life with great attention. Don't forget to call and invite your animal into everyday situations. Remember the new current of power that you felt when you held your animal for the first time. Let this power pervade you once in a while and it will become helpful in difficult or even dangerous situations, helping you to transform your fear. By calling on your ally, you can face the danger together, which will strengthen your instincts and allow you to act wisely.

Dance your animal as often as you can. Dusk in a forest is an especially powerful time because the nocturnal dwellers of the forest are awakening and will support you in your dance. Wear your power object while you are dancing; put the feather into your hair or wear the skin. Dance with eyes half closed and do not resist the motions of your ally; let them flow into you and feel what they have to offer you. You will often experience a totally new way of moving, standing or lying, one that will charge you with new energy and make you feel as if you could move mountains. You can use this in daily situations to your benefit when you feel lifeless and exhausted. Memorize all the images and pictures that come to your spiritual eye during the dance. All energies that are released during the dance will flow into your power object and charge it. Whenever you are talking or spending time with your friend, have the symbol ready and relate everything that is revealed to you to your object.

If you have urgent questions concerning your medicine, or questions that arise from certain dreams that you feel are important to understand, you can attempt a new journey into the realm of the animals. Initially there should always be someone with you to guide and help you. Drum and rattle are a must. Hold your power object on your fourth chakra. Before your descent into the realm of the animals, contact your ally, reveal your problem to it and ask it to guide you in the lower world and show you possible answers.

Give all the information that you discover during these journeys, as well as that received from dreams and dances, to your object. To do that, sit up and hold it above your fourth chakra. Go to the fourth chakra on your inhale, and push the information into your object on the exhale. These messages belong to your medicine. Also, meditate on your power object to check what powers it already carries. A good time to do this is during a full moon ritual.

Once you have decided to follow the path of the shaman, it will never be you who acts during rituals and ceremonies—you will always let your animal ally work through you. This way your work will carry the quality of magic: You will be open to the cosmic powers, and they will use you as their tool. This makes you a servant and assistant of the Whole.

The Power Song

In shamanic tradition you will find what is called the power song which can assist you in attracting your ally. This song becomes a magical or power song if its melody is not thought up by you, but instead is received from higher powers. To even perceive such a song, it is absolutely necessary to quiet your own melodies and become an empty resonant body for their song.

As usual, it is best to be close to a river, tree, or on a mountain-top where you can be alone with the entities that dwell there. Magical powers are strongest in the solitude of nature. It is also good to fast for this ritual. While you journey, let your way of moving be taken over by your animal friend; move the way it wants to and let it guide you until you feel its rhythm and your lips start forming sounds and syllables, words and a melody become apparent.

Power songs are usually very simple in words and melody; they may even seem monotonous. But that is good, because calling your ally with the song, singing it like a mantra while meditating, will put you in a kind of trance from where you can easily take the step into a shamanic state of consciousness. Sing the power song whenever you feel like it and whenever you want to call your allies.

Cooperation with Your Animal Ally
The Transmission of Power

Another ancient shamanic method of healing is to send power to someone—rudimentary fragments of that knowledge still roam our language, such as "cross your fingers" or "I will be thinking of you." We could think of innumerable situations when it would be helpful to send power to somebody. Imagine a friend who is very ill or in an otherwise critical situation and you want to send power to support the healing process. What would be the most effective way of doing that?

To transmit power you must understand that it is never "your" power that traverses the distance. That would be dangerous and harmful, because where energy balance is concerned, nobody is healthy and pure enough to attempt such a step without risk. You can only transmit energy from a source which is inherently inexhaustible and always in a state of equilibrium. To tap into a source like this, you need a mediator who can perform this task for you. This will be your animal ally. The same things it does to keep you healthy, it can do for someone else, given certain conditions. This is usually done by contacting the ally of the person concerned. It does not matter whether that person knows his or her ally or not; your ally knows whom to contact to make sure that the magic will work.

Perform the ritual of power transmission in a dark room, preferably at night. Cleanse yourself and the place where you will be working with smoke. Invoke the powers of the four directions and ask for their help too. Turn in the direction of your friend in need, close your eyes and perform the small death breathing: Breathe in for twelve seconds through your nose, hold for twelve seconds and breathe out intermittently for twelve seconds and hold again for twelve seconds—seven times in all.

Now visualize your friend as vividly as possible; let him or her come alive in your mind. This visualization establishes a link to the astral body of your friend—transmission of energy is possible only on this subtlest level of matter. The flux of energy settles in your friend's etheric body and any surplus will overflow and benefit all other areas of your friend's body-soul-spirit. Once you have achieved a clear picture of your friend in your mental eye, start calling your ally by singing your power song, accompanied by a drum or rattle. As soon as you feel your ally's presence, tell it your friend's full name, your friend's location and what he or she is suffering from; ask it to send as much power there as needed. Do not ask for anything else but this transmission of energy, and concentrate on the mental picture of your sick friend; do not lose it!

Once you have become more skilled, you will be able to see what kind of power transmission has happened; usually you will be able to see the way power flows to this mental image. It usually appears as an energy-filled pencil of light rays, visible on a specific part of the body, or you might even see the power animal of your friend come to support your ally.

The transmission of power should end after about ten minutes. In critical situations repeat this procedure several times a day, and in case of a prolonged disease, do it once a day.

Pay close attention to how you feel afterward. If you feel energized and vital you can be sure that it was not you who gave away power. But if you feel weakened, next time you will have to take care not to get involved in the healing process, regardless of your good intentions. Your involvement will not have any beneficial effects for you or your sick friend.

Power transmission knows no physical boundaries. It does not matter how far away the person in question is or how close. It can be done while you are in the same room. For example, someone is in a tense situation—he or she is in court or has to deliver a speech. If you are present, you can ask the allies to send power to this person by inwardly reciting this wish like a mantra. Cooperation with your animal friend becomes especially fruitful in professional situations. For example, you have to perform meticulous work with your hands, or you find yourself helpless in front of a classroom full of screaming kids who are paying no attention to you whatso-ever—you can handle innumerable situations better with the help of your animal ally.

Its help will be especially welcome if you work in the healing professions. Whenever you are touching the body of your patient with your hands, you should ask your ally to support you and guide your hands to the right spot or suggest the right words. Also consult it if you want to find the psychosomatic cause of a disease from which you or a friend suffer. It may be advisable to take your question with you on a new journey into the realm of the animals. "Down there" you can also inquire about the appropriate method of healing. Always request your ally to accompany you on these journeys and to lead you to the right "authorities."

If you like to paint, you can incorporate all the images that you have encountered on these journeys into a picture that you can meditate on later. Sit in your medicine wheel at the place of the west, the power of introspection. Put the picture you have drawn in front of you. Take your power object for additional support, and call your ally. Ask a friend to accompany you on a drum for about ten minutes, playing a continuous rhythm in common time (ONE-two-three-four). Contemplate your picture, and let yourself be carried into it by the rhythm of the drum until you actually feel yourself walking within the picture. Whenever you feel like it, or whenever you come across a symbol that you don't understand, call your ally for help; show it all the images that still seem like empty symbols to you and ask to know their hidden meaning. Continue this meditation until you have grasped the complete significance of the picture. You might also try to meditate in all four or even eight directions, asking their respective powers for help.

When human beings find their allies in the realm of the ani-mals, they also bear a new responsibility. They are responsible in the sense that they must be willing to join with this new power, making sure that it remains with them as an inexhaustible source of wisdom. The animal ally is not a pet to bring pleasure to the household, but a being which we, as humans, need for our growth

192

processes and to teach us as our personal master. As with all things, you have to be aware of the implications of each step that you take on this shamanic path of knowledge. It is a cosmic gift to be able to find an ally in the realm of the animals in the first place; therefore, it must not be treated thoughtlessly rather, it must be accepted in gratitude as a medicine that helps us to become Whole. There are so many situations where it would be helpful to feel this power and to harness oneself to it, yet the personal bond, cooperation and friendship will be different for everybody. If this spiritual alliance becomes neglected the ally will quickly leave. It is dependent on communication with human beings, kept alive through dance, dialogue, questions and requests for guidance.

Besides the journey into the realm of the animals there are other ways of finding your animal. The American Indians have a ritual called vision quest that requires the participant to stay alone in the wilderness for a few days and nights while fasting, praying and invoking the powers to ask them for medicine. Usually the animal will then appear to show the direction in which it may be found. Another way of finding the ally is by consuming magical plants and letting the spirit of the plants show the way to the animal. Or your benefactor from the animal world may simply appear, in a sudden vision that gives you power instantly.

This is the end of our discussion of the animal ally. I fully hope that you have found valuable hints and stimulus to pursue this exciting subject further.

The Medicine Shield

If you have found your three allies, and with their help have come to recognize your medicine more clearly, you can build yourself a medicine shield on which you can display your medicine in symbols and colors. In the tradition of shamanism this is an excellent exercise in keeping your medicine in mind. Shamans take a piece of leather, stretch it over a round frame of wood, and then paint it with personal symbols. It bears all the symbols that they have received in dreams, on vision quests and from other rituals. It includes all their plant, mineral and animal allies, plus other symbols that depict the shamans' medicine. Usually the medicine shield hangs in front of the door to show everyone what medicine this person has. During ceremonies or healing sessions, its bearers wear it like the shield of a warrior, or simply hold it up in front of them. As the shamans encounter new symbols during their lifetimes, they are added to the shield; or it can be completely changed as their medicine changes.

In Europe, remnants of this ancient tradition can be found in the shields of the various guilds of artisans that were hung from the May tree in the center of the village. The May tree tradition has its origins in the Cosmic Tree through which human beings had access to heaven and earth. The medicine of the people of the village was thus gathered around the May tree and through it, related to the Whole. Only those guilds whose artisans actually worked in a given village were allowed to place their shields on the May tree so that any stranger could instantly know which professions or medicines were available there.

The shamanic custodians of the medicine wheel always point out that it is important to redefine one's medicine at different stages of one's path. The ceremony of shield painting forces us to become "real," to position the symbols so unambiguously that they become an obvious guide and showpiece of ourself and lets others recognize immediately what our medicine is, in the same way the plow always reflects the occupation of the farmer.

Try to construct your shield yourself, and paint it with all your symbols. Display it in your home like a mirror that functions constantly as a reminder of your mission. You can also use a shield as the skin for your drum. This brings us to our next topic: The ceremonial drum, which helps you in all your shamanic activities and must become, along with the rattle, one of your allies.

Drum and Rattle
Two More Allies of Human Beings

In conjunction with the ritual searching for your animal ally we have discussed the effects of the drum and rattle. Let us review this quickly: The monotonous beating of the drum and the shaking of the rattle affects the neurons of the brain after a while. This enables us to enter alternate states of consciousness that can be called shamanic, magical, or simply higher states of consciousness. Only through this change in consciousness are human beings able to access the invisible world.

How can the ceremonial use of the drum and rattle open the other world for us? In the tradition of shamanism, drum and rattle are essential accessories which become the bridge to the other world. Here is a quotation from Mircea Eliade, the great researcher of shamanism:

> The drum has a role of the first importance in shamanic ceremonies. Its symbolism is complex, its magical functions many and various. It is indispensable in conducting the shamanic séance, whether it carries the shaman to the "Center of the World," or enables him to fly through the air, or summons and "imprisons" the spirits, or, finally, if the drumming enables the shaman to concentrate and regain contact with the spiritual world through which he is preparing to travel.

(Mircea Eliade, *Shamanism: Archaic Techniques of Ecstasy*, p. 168).

The same is true for the rattle. The center of the world lies within us; there we are one with both worlds, the visible and the invisible. And we will "fly through the air" if we are one with our spirit, who is a part of the eternal cosmos. We will "summon the spirits" if we are in contact with our allies in the realm of the plants, stones and animals, as well as our personal helpers in the universe whether they be our ancestors, saints or enlightened souls. All these beings exist—all we have to do is call them and ask for help and cooperation. And the drum and rattle help us in this entreaty.

Calling the Sacred Power
of the Medicine Wheel with the Drum

Go to the medicine wheel, sit down at the place that attracts you the most at that moment with your drum and/or rattle, with whose help you will call the other powers of the wheel.

• Start with the power of the east; the evocation of the sacred One, the power of the sun. Become aware of who you are calling, which power you are inviting. Start drumming a fast but steady rhythm (one-one-one-one) until you feel the power rising and are coupled with it.

• Then call the sacred Two; the power of the west, the power of introspection and intuition, the power of the will. The accompanying beat should be a 2/2 beat (ONE-two, ONE-two). Proceed to the sacred Three only if you feel the power within you.

• The evocation of the sacred Three; the power of the plants, the power of primary trust and innocence is done with a 3/4 beat (ONE-two-three, ONE-two-three), always accentuating the first beat.

• Evocation of the sacred Four; the power of the north, of the animals, the power of the mind and logic, is done with a 4/4 beat (ONE-two-three-four, ONE-two-three-four, and so on).

• Evocation of the sacred Five; the power of human beings, is done with a 5/4 beat (ONE-two-three-four-five, ONE-two-three-four-five). All other evocations are drummed relative to the Five.

• To evoke the sacred Six; the power of the southeast, the power of the ancestors, use the beat: ONE-two-three-four-five-ONE, ONE-two-three-four-five-ONE, and so forth. Be aware of the sacred Five merging with the sacred One to form the sacred Six, the power of the ancestors.

• To evoke the sacred Seven; the power of the southwest, the power of dreams, drum and/or rattle: ONE-two-three-four-five-ONE-two, ONE-two-three-four-five-ONE-two, and so forth. It is the sacred Five that merges with the sacred Two to form the sacred Seven.

• To evoke the sacred Eight; the power of the northwest, the power of the laws and cycles, drum: ONE-two-three-four-five-ONE-two-three, ONE-two-three-four-five-ONE-two-three and so forth. Remember, it is the sacred Five which merges with the sacred Three, the power of the plants, to form the power of the sacred Eight.

• To evoke the sacred Nine; the power of the northeast, the power of motion and medicine, drum: ONE-two-three-four-five-ONE-two-three-four, ONE-two-three-four-five-ONE-two-three-four, and so forth. It is human beings, the sacred Five, who merge with the power of the animals, the sacred Four, to form the sacred Nine.

• To evoke the power of the sacred Ten; the power of the Higher Self, drum: ONE-two-three-four-five-ONE-two-three-four-five, ONE-two-three-four-five-ONE-two-three-four-five, and so forth. It is the human being who merges with the human being to form the sacred Ten.

If you evoke the powers from the sacred One to the sacred Ten you will evoke the powers of the higher octave automatically. Be aware too of your chakras in this meditation. The 1/1 beat will reach your 1st chakra, the 2/2 beat will reach your 2nd chakra and so on.

You may use just the drum, just the rattle, or you may use both at the same time. Rattle and drum symbolize the sphere of the world. As soon as we take them into our hands, we signal our Oneness with the cosmos.

Making a Drum and Rattle

You should have a rattle in your medicine bag as one of your personal objects. You can make one from a pumpkin or a calabaza: Let the gourd dry out completely, and then cut the top open and scrape out the dried up interior. Cleanse the inside of it with smoke and fill it with twenty grains of dried rice, corn or beans. Stones or semiprecious gems are also suitable; use whichever you prefer. The number twenty is a reminder of the sacred number.

Use a strong piece of wood for a handle, perhaps from your favorite tree, and glue it into the opening. You can paint the symbols and signs of your medicine on it, and if you have a garden, you can even grow the gourd yourself.

The drum can be any drum, but you can also make one yourself if you are good at working with leather and wood. You might also consider custom ordering one which gives you the advantage of designing it to your specifications. The skin can be related to your power animal.

Drum and rattle are aids in every shamanic ceremony helping the participants to tune into the magical part of themselves. It invokes and "tunes up" the powers—we should use them often to let their sound resonate in our inner being. They are not nonsense, but sacred objects of power, deserving our attitude of respect.

The Circle of Laws

The smallest building block of nature, the atom, is connected to the universe in eight different directions. The eight sacred directions of the medicine wheel are the holistic powers that we all have to merge with if we want to become healthy and whole. This is the case for each individual, and the same holds true for the whole of society and the political structures of human communities. With the growth of the Age of Aquarius all ideological veils will drop away, and the long yearned for utopia will be able to unfold freely. A society will arise that is no longer uprooted and separated from the cosmic structure, but chooses as its inner core the structure of the sacred circle to reintegrate itself into the harmony of cosmic laws. The revelation of the sacred wheel by the Indians at the dawn of the Age of Aquarius has placed a special key into the hands of the entire human race.

The eight sacred directions are fundamental pillars for a holistic existence on earth. They are the gates to the nagual which complement our perception of reality through insights into the world of the spirits. Indians and other natural tribes still regulate the structure and order of their tribal life according to the great spirit, the power of the nagual. That is why their elders are called medicine men or medicine women. If they sit down in the sacred circle to administer justice, everything they judge and think about will be embedded in the universal laws. Their voice will be the voice of the Great Spirit, the voice of Oneness, bringing healing and medicine to the people.

The Germanic tribes designated a special place in nature as a holy place of justice. It was called the Thing, a circle of stones with a central pole pointing to Polaris, where the gods administered justice in the field of Ida. Today we must seat ourselves in this circle again to establish a vivid connection between our communal order and the universal order.

This may sound like daydreaming or even seem ridiculous to some, but before we judge, we should actually experience the original meaning of this circle of laws.

Every large society runs into difficulties in its communal life, and it is very difficult to find rules that govern the cohesion of the communities to everyone's satisfaction. A new, yet old way to deal with these problems is to heed the guidance of the circle of laws.

To enact the circle of laws, you will need sixteen persons sitting in pairs in the eight directions. In each direction there will be a man and a woman, except for the east, where you need two men, and in the west, where you need two women. There should be a tree in the center that prevents the opposite pairs from seeing each other. (If you are building a circle of laws within a room, a vase with a dense branch or a large plant will serve the purpose.) The opposite places are really meant to be opposites, which is especially apparent through the placement of two men in the east and two women in the west.

Distribution and Significance of the Eight Seats

The East
Place of the Sacred One and Eleven

In the east we find the proclaimers who will introduce to the circle the new, like a vision. This may be a problem, an idea, or a creative suggestion that has importance for the community or something that the community has requested be viewed from all angles by its representatives. The two men in the east are called *heyokas* (the "holy fools") by the western Indians. They are wise and have insight. To reinforce working with opposites, they word the subject matter in a reverse fashion. For example, if the suggestion were made that everybody with a lot of money should support those with no money, the heyokas would then say: "Everybody with money should use it to their hearts' content and not worry about any poor people."

The Southeast
Place of the Sacred Six and Sixteen

The first answer to the problem comes from here. The advocates of history sit here; they base their arguments on historical knowledge. They are the philosophers, the educated, those in possession of all available knowledge. They talk to the representatives to their left in the place of the south, the place of the sacred Three and Thirteen. As usual, the movement is clockwise and follows the path of the sun.

The South
Place of the Sacred Three and Thirteen

In the place of the south we have the "entrepreneurs" or, as they are called in tribal language, "warriors." Their task is the agreement of motivations and needs of the community with the problem to ensure the community's further growth. They talk to the place of the southwest.

The Southwest
Place of the Sacred Seven and Seventeen

Here we find the medicine people, the healing priests. Their position regarding the problem takes into account the emotional and mental well-being of the whole community, the dream of Humankind. They talk to the women in the west.

The West
Place of the Sacred Two and Twelve

The west is the place of the women. They take care that nothing will be done that harms the children. The new of the east, which is introduced by the heyokas, has to be integrated in such a way that it will not harm the earth or any of its inhabitants. The women talk to the northwest.

The Northwest
Place of the Sacred Eight and Eighteen

The politicians and councillors sit here. They are responsible for relating the problem to the wisdom of the great cycles and laws of the universe. They talk to the north.

The North
Place of the Sacred Four and Fourteen

Here we find the workers and consumers. They work to integrate the new into the status quo. They talk to the northeast.

The Northeast
Place of the Sacred Nine and Nineteen

Here we find the lawyers and the whole of the judicial system. They summarize all arguments and statements made so far and define the new law from that. They talk to the heyokas who do not make any further comments themselves.

Now the draft of the new law must be brought to a vote. Altogether there are fourteen voters because the heyokas are not allowed to vote. The women are in the majority because there are eight women and six men. Indians explain this circumstance with the fact that we live on the earth which is our Great Mother and female power. It is the most important power and must have priority in the natural giving of laws.

A law is legally binding if it receives eleven out of fourteen votes. This is a natural proportionality of life; one in which a harmonic equilibrium can still be guaranteed. It is exactly the acid-base ratio in the chemical make-up of the human body: $11:14 = 0.789$. It basically means that even if there is one-fifth disagreement, it cannot throw the Whole out of balance; it can be integrated without problem.

If you consider a problem that concerns the public in this way, you will reach surprising solutions that could not have been found without the help of the circle. If we consider and view a problem from all directions it becomes possible to illuminate it with complete consciousness.

I would like to send the concept of the circle of laws into the public as an alternative vision for politicians and parliamentarians with the hope that some day the representatives of a new society will sit down in a circle to connect the divine wisdom and cosmic order with our earthly affairs.

PART IV

RITUALS-A WAY OF HEALING

Our life is full of rituals and ritualistic actions. All human cultures reflect this. But in all cultures there is a fine line between habit and ritual. A habit is a ritual that has lost its inner meaning and is just practiced mechanically. It therefore gives no energy to the doer as the original ritual once did. The original purpose of a ritual was always holy, in the sense that it healed and allowed Man to participate in the Whole.

A ritual or ceremony has an inner course of events which is a legacy from our forebears, or may be determined by whoever leads the ceremony. Besides some new and many very old traditional ceremonies, there are innumerable nonmaterial ones that already exist in the realm of ideas, waiting to be manifested.

A ritual is a celebration of all life. In a ritual we can pledge or express gratitude; it is a bridge joining heaven and earth creating a stairway for our divine helpers to descend. A ceremony urges us to give symbolic form to what is contained in our spirits. It helps us to "bring our dream to earth," to materialize our spirit and to measure this embodiment against the eternal spirit.

Generally, a ritual is intended for the entire community so all can draw fresh power for their growth. Every ceremony that a community performs together has a certain agreed upon and understood theme. The individuals conform to this theme, understanding that they are equals in their common surrender to it. The ritual therefore becomes a unifying power, stimulating the entire community.

This is why more rituals survive in villages and small communities rather than in large cities where life is split into so many contradictory parts that it becomes impossible to trace individual relationships to the Whole.

Within our culture we know Christian rituals best: celebration of the holy Mass, baptism, marriage, funerals and religious festivals. But for many Christians these festivals are no longer "open," meaning their original significance has been lost. Early Christianity condemned many ancient rituals as heathenistic or idolatrous and exerted great skill and effort to erase all traces of the "devil's work." In many cases where pre-Christian rituals could not be extinguished, they were distorted beyond recognition so that nothing remained of their original significance. Only then were they integrated into the new religion.

The individual was subjected to religious tutelage, and the church achieved omnipotence over its members by regulating the connection of each individual to the divine source with binding dogmas. This complicated the essential inner participation of the individual with the ritual. But we must give contemporary Christianity its due. There are more priests attempting to return to the sources of the original symbols, opening them up, allowing individual participation once more and thus becoming a true sharing.

Rituals must be understandable, and their symbolism significant to every participant. If only the leader of the ceremony has insight into its deeper meaning, all others will be excluded from the healing force that should pour forth on everyone.

Now, in the age of Aquarius, since we no longer accept the Redeemer's connection to God as a substitute for our own, it becomes vital to remember the original power of ritual. Now everyone has the opportunity to celebrate life, alone or with others, without the need for a special ritual leader belonging to a specific sect or religion. Everyone can be self-sufficient without the need of a representative of God, because God works with every person seeking spiritual communion.

The following contemporary ceremonies and rituals will help to make our theme a little more understandable. They should also give us healing energy because they are oriented toward the Whole. All rituals can be celebrated alone, but they may also be enriched by the participation and sharing of others.

Balancing and Cleansing Ceremonies

Illness and dissension are definite signs that the trinity of the human essence, the structure of body-soul-spirit, is out of balance. It means that we are no longer in natural, harmonious vibration with the Whole, but of our own volition have become "outlaws" in the universal order.

The religious orientation of human beings toward the Whole is our golden center and guide for all our actions in life. We have a strong tendency to forget our center and this is evident in the positioning of our four shields. This forgetfulness expresses itself in negative emotions such as suffering, sorrow, fear, hate, jealousy, envy, dissatisfaction, helplessness, injustice, and so forth.

To help us return to our centers and stabilize our beings, we can use cleansing or balancing rituals. They date back to ancient times, yet knowledge of them has not been lost because there have always been those whose medicine was the keeping of and passing on of ancient wisdom. Through the revelation of shamanic wisdom we have the opportunity to unite with the original power of these rituals.

The Spiral

The spiral is a very old symbol. It is found on all historic sites of initiation wherever they are still preserved. The most famous might be the one near Nazca in Peru which extends over several miles. In nature as well we find an abundance of spiral forms: snails, seashells, and the leaves of certain ferns; and in the human body, DNA, the auditory canal and even the fetal position remind us of a spiral. What wisdom is hidden in the spiral? Where does its shape come from?

The path of the sun as seen from earth provides an answer to these questions. The sun moves from its highest point, the summer solstice, down to its lowest, the winter solstice. As we know, the sun does not simply reverse direction when it moves upward again, but keeps moving in the same direction—therefore, it must cross the path it took in its last revolution. This movement results in an elongated spiral.

This spiral movement revealed the wisdom of eternal life and the secret of death and rebirth to the ancients. The initiates of this wisdom understood the infinitely spiraling sun as a mirror for their own lives. The Sun, the Great Father, is reborn on the day of his death, the winter solstice, to move into a new cycle of life whose fruit will ripen at its highest point, the summer solstice, only to die and be harvested to make room for a new birth. It taught the ancients about the infinitely finite cycles of life.

The spiral is the eternally turning wheel of death and rebirth around a motionless hub. In its emptiness, this quiet center is the primal source of all possibilities of life and the prime origin of all its actual forms. Around the center is empty space that reaches out into infinity—the permanent turning of the spiral. This very center, which gives the impulse of motion to the spiral, is found also present within human beings. It gives us the capacity to comprehend everything in its basic form and to receive and absorb everything that contains the Whole. The spiral also reminds us of the law: "As above, so below."

If you could see people in the light of their auras, you would know that we look like illuminated eggs. Within this aura, energy moves in a spiral fashion; it forms an upper and lower cone that touch each other at their base. This base is our center.

The Ceremony of the Spiral

Construction and Use

Building the spiral for the first time is a ritual in itself. Look for a place in the wilderness, or in your yard, where you can build a spiral about sixteen to eighteen feet in diameter. Choose a powerful spot, a place with positive energy, as the center. You can call on your allies to awaken your intuition and instincts to help you feel the call of the right spot. Or, you can use a pendulum, which will start to rapidly rotate clockwise and thus reflect the positive energy of a given spot, or you can enlist the aid of a diviner.

The next task is to collect stones; you will need enough to lay out a spiral that fills your circle. You should collect the stones in a shamanic way, informing them of what they are needed for and leaving some tobacco in gratitude. First mark the center and the four cardinal points, the east, the west, the south and the north on the outermost line of the spiral. Then, as you move inward, do the same for the second round, and so on. Leave about two feet between the lines. After you have laid out the cardinal points, connect them with smaller stones starting from the center until you reach the entrance which must point to the north.

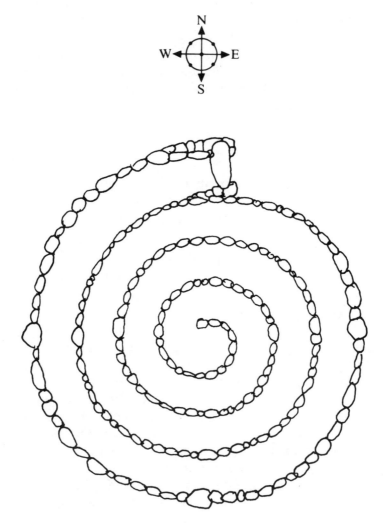

The entrance (or exit) has to be built with larger stones placed one atop the another, two high, serving as pillars to support an elongated "gate stone" to seal the spiral when you are not using it. The layout of the spiral on the ground creates a holy space and represents the spiral's motion. Imagine two cones of energy with their tips meeting at the center of the spiral, as though it were an hour glass with the lower half buried in the earth. The cone with its tip pointing upward concentrates earthly energy on the spiral, and the cone with its tip directed downward concentrates cosmic energy. The spiral extends unbounded within these cones.

Now you must awaken the power of the spiral. Call the powers of the sacred directions and the power of the sacred center to awaken them. Use your smoke bowl or smudge stick, face all the directions and call out loud. Send your voice into the universe along with the smoke. Then, walk the spiral once until you reach the center, cleanse it with smoke and dedicate it. Once you have reached the center, call the sacred power of the Great Mother and Great Father and ask them to join you in the center. Continue fanning cleansing smoke as you leave.

This will dedicate and awaken the spiral, which is now ready to transmit power to all those taking part in the ritual. If several people are participating, one of them should play the drum: ONE-two-ONE, ONE-two-ONE, and so forth, while the others repeat the mantra "UMA KON." UMA and the drum beat One-two mean the earth; KON and the drum beat One mean the heavens. Drumming and reciting this ancient mantra, which originated in the Quetchua of the Inca, provoke the merger of the earthly powers (UMA) with the heavenly powers (KON).

While all other participants stand outside and around the spiral, intoning the mantra to the beat of the drum, one participant goes inside the spiral, making sure to step in left foot first. The way your spiral is laid out you can only enter it in a counterclockwise direction. This causes the discharge of disturbing energies into the earth, where they are transformed into positive energy. Once you have reached the center of the spiral, turn first to the west and raise both arms. Inhale twice, deeply, to absorb the power of the earth.

Then turn counterclockwise, look to the east, to the power of the Sun, and breathe in with raised arms to absorb this power. Remain in the center as long as you feel attracted by this exchange of power. Meditate on this power of the center, keeping in mind that here you are in contact with your own center.

The center is the source of life, pervading all its forms in a spiral motion as an energizing and creative current. It is like a network of subtle energy that links everything there is. As you leave the spiral, you are walking clockwise which will charge you positively. Through these changes in the movement of energy you will experience a kind of energetic rebalancing that will last the whole day. This makes it a good ritual to celebrate at sunrise, enabling you to meet the demands of the day, at rest in your center.

After the last participant has gone through the spiral, it should be closed with the "gate stone" that you lay across the pillars at the entrance. This will end the ritual as well. If you are performing the ritual by yourself, you can recite the mantra UMA KON inwardly, or use drums as a "tuning in" before you enter the spiral.

The Sweat Lodge:
The Ceremony of Death and Rebirth

The sweat lodge ceremony is communal, and it is celebrated by almost all peoples of the earth. What remains of the sweat lodge in the urbanized western world is the sauna or steam bath, used for the cleansing of the body. But in its original, ritualistic use, the sweat lodge ceremony is a holistic cleansing ritual that purifies body-soul-spirit, washing away old burdens and dirt (these are aspects of death), and filling us with fresh energy (aspects of rebirth). The ritual is still performed today in this spirit; and with the revelation of the medicine wheel by the shamans of the North American Indians, it has regained the true splendor of its wholeness.

A sweat lodge building consists basically of a plaited basket standing upside down on the ground. This small wigwam is made of bent twigs of willow anchored into the ground at the points of the eight sacred directions. It is then covered with blankets and mats until it becomes completely dark inside. A hole about three feet deep is dug in the center to hold hot stones during the ceremony.

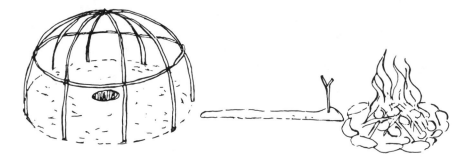

The entrance of the sweat lodge is to the east. Outside, about five paces away from the entrance, is a fireplace where the stones are heated until they are red-hot. From the entrance of the sweat lodge to the fireplace a narrow path is layed out that opens into a circular place close to the fire. This path bears the name "Way of the heart." During the ceremony, the spiritual power of the universe and all its beings flows along it. Place a forked branch in the center of the circle at the end of the path to symbolize the eternal love-embrace between primordial mother and primordial father and to remind us that only the path of love and surrender can give us this unity with our Higher Self.

As we enter the sweat lodge, its low entrance forces us to crawl like little children. The sweat lodge symbolizes the womb of our Great Mother Earth. The fire in the east symbolizes our Great Father Sun whose seed is the glowing stones. If the participants crawl into the sweat lodge as naked as they were made by their parents, the Sun and the Earth, the entrance becomes a vagina whereby they enter the womb of the Great Earth Mother. Call out before entering: "For all my ancestors and relatives!" in recognition of our link with the Great Cosmic Family, in which humans are just children of the Sun, like the stones, plants, animals and our ancestors who accompany us as close spiritual relatives.

The red-hot stones are brought from the fire place to the pit in the sweat lodge. This symbolizes the moment of conception: The seed of the sun penetrates the womb of the earth. We, their children, watch our own conception and are reborn upon leaving the lodge at the end of the ceremony.

An experienced initiate of the ritual, one who can lead it responsibly, should always be present during the ceremony in the sweat lodge. The same holds true during the construction of the lodge which is a sacred act. Each movement reflects a certain power that must be explained to everyone participating in the building process: the cutting of the twigs, their placement in the sacred directions and their connections—the one in the east must be bent over to the west, the one in the south is bent to the north and so on; the digging of the fire pit; the collecting of the stones; covering the interior of the lodge with ferns. All these are meaningful gestures that the leader of the ritual must be able to explain to the participants.

The ceremony is usually held at night. The night supports the opening of our senses to the nagual. It seems to strip off and dissolve our material garment, gives wings to our spirit and carries it to its true home, the realm of wisdom and vision.

The stones have to be heated in the fire of the east about two hours before the beginning of the ceremony. One of the participants must be responsible for this—the "fire man" or "fire woman." You will need about twenty one-pound stones and plenty of wood. Starting and tending the fire and heating the stones is an important part of the ceremony. It is a sacred act, for it is a prayer to the power of the fire and the stones and a pledge to help cleanse all those in the sweat lodge and to give them new life. Gratitude is expressed to our relatives, the stones for sacrificing themselves for this ceremony, as well as to the trees who gave their wood for this purpose.

To enforce the fire's cleansing and transforming power, put sage into the flames. As soon as the fire is burning, the participants should gather around the fire, meditatively tuning in to the ceremony. This is done most beautifully in the medicine wheel, where the order of sitting in the sweat lodge can be determined beforehand. All participants must be cleansed with smoke.

Just before the start of the ceremony, the women who are present dedicate and awaken the lodge. (It is done by women because their wombs make them closer to the spirit of the lodge.) The interior must be cleansed with smoke of sage, lavender and Arbor vitae. The sacred powers of the medicine wheel are invoked and requested to come to the center of the lodge.

The sweat lodge ceremony can have a certain theme; for example, the dedication of the lodge to the south, making it a "lodge of the south," where you pray for emotional stability, harmony and trust. Or you can dedicate it to another direction, as a "dream-lodge" or "animal-lodge." The powers must be informed about these special requests, and asked for cooperation and support.

The women will then cleanse the exterior of the lodge with smoke after invoking the powers of the four cardinal directions to dissipate disturbing influences.

Now the sweat lodge has become a sacred space and is ready to receive you. The participants take all their clothes off and take only a towel to sit on. Everyone is allowed to take one object into the lodge for the purpose of charging it during the ritual. Any movement made inside the lodge must be clockwise, and the fire in the center may never be crossed. Upon entering, everyone must say: "For all my ancestors and relatives." Once everyone is sitting around the fire pit in a circle, the leader enters and sits in the place of the east, whose power will guide the ceremony. Behind the leader, the keeper of the fire closes the lodge with a blanket to prevent any light from entering.

At first everyone is silent, absorbing the darkness and energy present in the circle. Keep your eyes open and look into the darkness, the nothingness. The leader will then ask the fire keeper to bring in some stones. As soon as the glowing stones are in the fire pit, the leader tosses sage and other herbs over them creating a pleasant scent which spreads throughout the lodge. Before the entrance is closed again, the keeper of the fire gives a jug of water, preferably pure spring or river water, to the leader. The leader will pour the first water on to the hot stones, the "salutary infusions," and will call the Great Mother and the Great Father and the powers of the four directions, asking them for their presence and assistance, pouring water after each invocation.

Hot steam is noisily rising from the stones, bodies start sweating, and the heat is increasing after each infusion; it may become somewhat exhausting as the breathable air becomes thinner, but all this helps you push yourself to your limits, and then beyond.

The ritual is divided into four rounds, one for each of the four directions. The first round is the path of the south. All participants express their most intimate and important wishes for themselves, that which they think they need most for fulfillment, harmony of soul and for prime trust in life. Everyone speaks their wishes aloud, as personal prayers to the powers of the universe who are all present in that small space. Every prayer is accompanied by an infusion. With the completion of the first round, the ritual leader may ask for fresh stones if necessary.

Then follows the second round, the way of the west. Here you plead for your fellow human beings, for the concerns of your friends and request the healing of the earth. Prayers are spoken in turn, and each prayer is followed by an infusion.

Between the second and third round there may be a pause, giving participants the opportunity to crawl outside and lie in the damp grass for a little while and watch the stars. It is a wonderful experience to lie naked and feel yourself embedded in the rhythm of nature, free of all burden, feeling your own life force pulsating in unison with the currents of the universe.

After everyone is seated back in the sweat lodge, the leader gets fresh stones and starts the third round, the way of the north. All think of what they can "let go" of and what is currently keeping them from feeling healthy and whole, what disturbs their balance and distracts them from recognizing and fulfilling their missions. This may be jealousy, envy, self-doubt, hate, guilt, sorrow, expectations, unessential desires and so on. But physical pains can be let go of as well, for example, an affliction that you no longer need to learn from because you have already integrated its message into your wisdom.

Letting go is one of the most important parts of the entire ceremony because it is at this time that transformation occurs: The old dies and the new can unfold. Letting go has to come from the depths of your heart, as in the power of the animals who sacrifice themselves as nourishment for us. It is a promise to Mother Earth that you have to keep. That is why you should give away only those things that you really don't need to learn from any more. All things that throw us out of balance and cause us sorrow are props that help us grow if we are ready to accept them. Everything that we let go of the earth absorbs and lovingly transforms into something new that benefits us as an influx of power. Letting go transforms hindrances that we may attain our goals.

In this round too, everything is spoken aloud. Nothing is hidden and everyone participates in the weaknesses and deficiencies of the others, and through this sharing, a bond and unity arises because each person is a mirror for the others. Usually this round is the most exhausting one. You can really feel the waves of power surging through the lodge, intercepting and transforming the energy.

For the fourth and last round, new stones will again be brought in. The way of the east will be celebrated in silence. The leader gives twenty infusions for the twenty sacred powers of the universe, the healing power of the Whole. All participants go within and listen to the voice of the universe that speaks to them twenty times. The fire of the east gives light, inspiration and creativity, which translates into spiritual power to everyone. The heat rises rapidly due to the many infusions and often becomes unbearable. It is good to learn to surrender and fall into this heat without resistance. The "falling into" is the small death that you must willingly die to experience your rebirth. It is an incredibly delightful feeling to go through this phase of absolute physical exhaustion, to exceed your limits, and cross the boundaries to a new and unknown land into which you will be reborn, once you leave the womb of Mother Earth. Body-soul-spirit are cleansed, transformed and charged with cosmic power—a new life can start!

After the ceremony, all participants share the experiences and discoveries of their journey and a delicious meal, if desired.

The Rituals
of the Four Elements

The four elements: the fire of the east, the earth of the west, the water of the south and the air of the north, are the four basic building blocks of life that we can discover and celebrate in the following ceremonies.

The Fire Ritual

This ceremony is a communal celebration, but it can also be performed alone. For a group ceremony, a leader with experience in the fire ritual should be chosen who can protect all participants. You will need a good fireplace. It can be an open fireplace in your home, but it is probably better to have a fire pit outside. In the shamanic way, the participants gather plenty of wood and a bundle of green twigs. Herbs for cleansing with smoke, a quart of olive oil, and some pleasing scent oil are needed as well.

The ceremony is held in the evening, after dark. The inner preparation of the participants starts some two hours earlier. The leader explains the preparatory exercise: All participants think of something essential, a basic request, that they need for their medicine and a personal weakness that may now be let go of. For this exercise it is best to go into a forest, or if the ceremony is held in town, a park or garden. There, everyone gives form to their requests and weaknesses by writing them on a piece of paper and attaching it to a branch or by carving them on a piece of wood. The symbol, whatever it is, must be flammable.

Once all participants have gathered, the leader creates a sacred space. If the ritual is held at home around your fireplace, everyone sits in a half circle; if it is held outside, a full circle is formed around the fire. The place should be cleansed with smoke, and the powers must be invoked. Seal the circle (or half circle) by walking around it and fanning it with smoke, or sprinkling water or tobacco. Then everyone is ritually cleansed with smoke, as are the fireplace and the wood. The leader of the ritual lights the fire. For the fire to be a "holy fire" and a healing power, its spiritual power has to be invoked and awakened.

Indian shamans have a special song that requests the Spirit of the Fire to come into the earthly, ceremonial fire. They call the fire spirits, the fauns and salamanders, and ask them to put the fire into a favorable mood so it causes no damage, and to give them the power of purification and transformation. One or more people should play the drums in the rhythm of the sacred One and the sacred Two so fire and earth can become one. (ONE-ONE-two; ONE-ONE-two). The others can support the rhythm with a rattle or by clapping.

It would be wonderful to find your own song for the invocation of the fire spirits that all participants can join in singing. It can be short and simple, and should have the power of a mantra rather than artistic value. In the meantime, the leader tends the fire and calls the power of the sun, asking it to be present during the ceremony. The leader gives scented oils to the flames to attract the fire spirits. The following is a possible invocation for attracting the spirits of the fire.

> *In the name of the element of fire*
> *and its blazing glow*
> *I call you, Salamanders!*
> *By the power of my magical will,*
> *fire spirits of friendly intentions,*
> *come here,*
> *and dedicate this fire with your power.*

It is important that the leader explain all these actions to the participants so they can grasp their meaning and not remain half-hearted spectators. This ritual needs the power and commitment of everyone. ("It needs the power of a heart," said a Peruvian medicine man.) That is why all must concentrate on the dedication of the fire. Sometimes one of the fire spirits appears, or the fire speaks, using its own signs and images that appear in the flames. The leader must pay attention to the signals from the fire to know when the dedication is complete. Then the leader can place his or her hands into the fire, draw power and be charged.

When the leader's hands can be put into the flames without being burned, then the fire spirits are there and their intentions are friendly. But if the leader's hands are rejected by the destructive flames, continued offerings and invocations must be made until the flames are no longer harmful.

When this is achieved, olive oil is poured into the flames and the fire is asked to receive all the participants. The leader starts by kneeling down in front of the fire with his or her symbolic object and talking to the Spirit of the Fire: The leader's wish and weakness are told to the fire and to the others, and the fire is requested to accept the request, fulfill the wish and to transform the weakness into strength. The symbol is then placed in the flames and watched to see how it is accepted by them.

Sometimes the fire is upset and throws the object back out ("Your prayer did not come from the heart") or it is happy and emits a lot of sparks. The fire might also make a lot of smoke to show a certain direction, or a face or image will become visible. All these things contain answers to be interpreted.

The leader then thrusts his or her hands three times into the fire, the first time drawing the power of the fire and transferring it to the first chakra; the second time transferring the power to the fourth chakra; and the third time transferring it to the sixth chakra, the third eye. The leader thanks the fire and makes room for the person to the left.

Going clockwise, all participants approach the fire in this way. It may happen that some are rejected by the fire and cannot put their hands into the flames without being hurt. This may happen for several reasons: Either the person's concern is not honest and does not come from the heart, they are trying to let go of a weakness too early, or their wish is not essential for their medicine. It is the duty of the leader to watch all this closely and to give the right advice or direction. Often a talk with those persons at the end of the session is helpful.

Once the last person has been with the fire, the leader closes the ritual with a gift of gratitude to the fire spirits—scented oil or sweet liqueur—and finally the bundle of green twigs is put into the flames to say good-bye to the fire and to receive a final message, hidden in the column of smoke that will rise from the flames.

The smoke may drift in a definite direction, may rise vertically, or hover close to the ground. All these are hints that should be kept in mind during the next few days. For example, the power of direction that the smoke drifts into should be meditated upon and contact with it should be consciously maintained. Only after the smoky signs have faded does the leader put water on the embers and make the sign of the four directions, so the energy of the cere-monial site can return to its original state. This closes the ritual.

The Earth Ritual

The Earth ritual is for healing purposes, and should only be attempted by someone familiar with shamanic healing procedures. It is especially effective for diseases of the bones, such as rheumatism, arthritis, bone atrophy and deformation, but also for cancer and muscular atrophy. At the same time it will have a healing effect on all emotional illnesses. For example, it is helpful for people who have difficulties working out their relationship with their parents; for those who have lost their willpower or those who do not have both feet anchored in the power of the earth. It can be used also for people we call insane (shamans would say "living too much in the nagual," being unable to reestablish their bond with the tonal). Generally this ritual means healing for everybody, because there are few who have a healthy relationship to the earth and who understand the dream that they are supposed to realize upon it.

For the earth ritual, the patient (or one being acted upon) must be buried in the ground usually for several hours, or even an entire day or night. This requires extensive preparation! The site should be in the wilderness and free of pollution of any kind. Spring or river water should be available in the immediate vicinity. It is very important to be able to work at the site without disturbance.

First the site must be dedicated by walking off a big circle and fanning it with cleansing smoke. The ceremony will take place inside this circle. The leader calls the powers of the sacred directions and asks them to be present and helpful during the healing session. The patient, if able to do so, should dig the hole alone. The hole should be about two feet deep and the length of the patient's body, and the bottom should be covered with ferns or fresh leaves. These help to withdraw negative energy from the patient. Then the hole must be thoroughly cleansed with smoke. The patient must be put into the hole naked. If a certain chakra is concerned, a crystal can be placed there, if the leader is familiar with crystal medicine. Then the patient is covered gently with soil or sand until completely embedded in the earth with only his or her head exposed. The patient's neck must be well supported to avoid cramps.

It is good to have three helpers who sit around the "grave" to the west, south and north. The leader sits to the east and is guided by the power of inspiration. The three helpers channel the energy of the other powers toward the leader.

At the beginning of the healing session, the leader calls the power of the Great Mother Earth and asks with these or similar words: "Into your strong arms and fertile womb I entrust this child of yours. I beg you, take it and give (him or her) what (he or she) needs to trust you again and take away what stops (him or her) from living (his or her) dream."

Then the leader calls the spirits of the earth, the gnomes, dwarfs and gremlins, and informs them in a loud voice of the objective of the healing and requests them to help with the transformation of the patient. Within the cosmic metabolism, it is the duty of the spirits of the earth to channel ethereal-electrical currents of energy to the stones, minerals and sand which the patient will feel as wavelike vibrations on a cellular level. These have a healing effect throughout the entire body-soul-spirit system, wherever healthy energy currents are blocked. (Some shamans are able to perceive this wavelike energy as concentric circles of iridescent light that emit wonderful harmonies.) The buried patient will have to breathe strongly at first. The leader can help the patient to not resist the earth, but rather to surrender and fall into her, by doing certain breathing exercises together.

The patient is entrusted to the Earth, our true mother, and if she is surrendered to, she will reveal the necessary steps for the healing process. The one who is buried in the earth will probably go through some fear and relive old sufferings and painful situations; but being linked to the earth, the patient can see things with different eyes and understand the meaning of these sufferings. The leader will be able to recognize the patient's transformation from personal involvement to a neutral, holistic point of view when the tears have dried and are replaced with the appearance of enraptured radiance on the patient's face.

Whoever participates in the ceremony as a helper will be able to perceive the various fluctuations of energy caused by the earth's healing, transforming force. It may take several hours until the patient experiences the process of total dissolving. The patient can then no longer sense the boundaries of the body, and gets the feeling that the body is disintegrating cell by cell, melting finally into the body of the earth. This is an important but dangerous moment in the healing process that demands the utmost care and attention from the leader and helpers. Special attention has to be given to the patient's breathing which is endangered in the experience of dissolution, and seems like dying to the buried patient.

The experience of dying will be unforgettable for the patient. The saying "Dust unto dust" will become a living truth. In the depth of this experience, the patient discovers the gift of rebirth, of renewal, and it will unmistakably show on his or her face as great happiness and luminous radiance. After some time, when the patient is ready to be "freed" of the grave, the digging out will begin. This must be done extremely slowly and with great care to let the buried person feel how the body gradually gains back its shape, as if it were being reconstructed, so to speak.

A terrible stench will ooze out of the grave when the body is unearthed. This is a clear sign that an actual material transformation has occurred. Once the body is completely exposed it has to be given some time to absorb oxygen. Standing up is a critical moment. It is best to have the patient assume the fetal position while still lying on the ground and then roll onto the knees and gradually assume a crouching position. Then the leader grasps the patient under the arms and carefully helps him or her up.

In the perception of the patient this process again reflects the experience of rebirth: Newly born, the patient emerges from the womb of the mother with the innocence and trust of a child. The patient must be accompanied to the spring or river and carefully washed clean. The open pit must be sprinkled with water.

The spirits of the earth should be thanked for their help with coins or glittering ribbons that are buried in the hole as it is filled. This closes the outer form of the ritual. The leader or healer should talk to the patient afterward to discuss the particular stages of the healing process, and later lend support with word and deed because often the time following this ritual is a period of change and transformation for the patient.

The Water Ritual

The human body consists of almost 70 percent water. The attractive power of the earth, gravity, exerts itself primarily upon this substance, and thus water becomes the basis of our gravitational mooring to the earth. Water is an absolutely essential element of life and cleanses and rejuvenates life's inner fluids.

From a ceremonial point of view, water has always played a cleansing role, cleansing the soul of Mankind. In the Christian ritual of baptism a small portion of the original essence of the water ritual is still alive. It is said that the newborn human being is washed free of original sin with baptism. But what is the meaning of the term original sin, stripped of its dogmatic implications? Sin means separate, to be separate from the original Oneness. By virtue of our very birth, we fall from a spiritual and universal state of consciousness into a material state, thus committing a sin.

This is the true meaning of original sin: it is the separation, the polarity and the path of discovery that is the heritage of humanity. The water of baptism is holy water that heals by pervading us with the power of the eternally flowing current of life. It also reminds us that within us too flows the eternal, the immortal: the spirit that never fell from the universal Oneness. We remain whole in the realm of our spirits, and with the help of our souls, it is possible to spiritualize our material bodies and merge with the Whole, even while we are here on earth. The shaman works with the cleansing power of water as a means of reuniting human beings with the Whole.

The water ritual described here should be celebrated communally. It is best to choose a running body of water for a ceremonial site, such as a river shallow enough to stand in. The first thing the leader of the ceremony does is dedicate the site by cleansing it with smoke. The participants, covered only with towels, form a circle in the water. They too must be cleansed with smoke.

To meditatively tune into the ritual, everyone stands facing upstream and tries, with eyes closed, to completely absorb the feeling of the friction and resistance of the water. Then all meditate silently on where they themselves feel their own resistance, on where their personal power is restricted and cannot flow freely, on where they themselves feel pressure and friction. Then everyone turns around and stands with their feet pointing in the direction of the flow, with eyes closed, just absorbing this physical feeling. Subsequently, each one meditates on the power of flowing: Where have I encountered flow in my life recently? How do I flow in the same way? To meditate means to listen to the inner, to silence your thoughts and let the water speak during the ritual as the power of eternal flowing.

After this tuning in, the ritual leader calls the sacred powers of all directions, especially the power of the south, the power of the water. The leader requests the spirits of the water, the undines and nixes to support the ceremony. Then, one after the other, each participant steps forward into the center of the circle to receive the spiritual elixir of life through "baptism." Everyone speaks in turn to the spirits of the water and tells them where they feel resistance and inability to flow, and requests the water to join them to its eternal flow.

Then the leader, the "baptist," takes a large feather, dips it into the water and brushes gently over the eyes of the person to be baptized, dips it in again and brushes over both ears, dips it in again and wets the nose, mouth, tongue and palms of the hands. Thereby reminding everyone to join their five senses to the current of the flowing spirit, to awaken spiritually and to merge the visible with the invisible. Finally, the leader takes a small bowl, fills it with water and pours it over the seventh chakra, through which we receive our dreams. If the leader is also working with crystal medicine, a crystal can be dipped into the water and used to balance the seventh chakra with thirteen circular movements.

Once all are baptized, the ritual should be closed with an expression of thankfulness to all present powers, and a gift of coins, pearls or perfume given to the water spirits.

The Air Ritual

The air is another elixir of life. We are in constant exchange with it through our breathing. Using conscious breathing, we can discover how we are really breathed into by the universal cosmic breath that pervades all life and encloses each link in the universe within its chain of breath. This chain of breath introduces us to the universal network of relationships between everything there is. It enables us to make contact with all life, and with our origin, through conscious breathing.

For the ceremony of the air, it is best to find a site that already has an airy feeling about it, like a mountaintop or the top of a tree. For the following ritual, a stately treetop was chosen as the ceremonial site. This ritual can be performed communally or alone. All participants look for a suitable tree; once it has been found, ask it if it wants to serve you for a few hours. Listen carefully for its answer. Once you have received a clear yes, cleanse the tree with smoke, always moving clockwise, and invoke the powers of the sacred directions, especially the power of the north, the power of the air and the wind. Also call the spirits of the air, the sylphs and trolls, and request them to support you.

Now climb up the tree and find a place where you can stand or sit safely. Take a few deep breaths. To tune in, drum a relatively fast and steady 4/4 beat (ONE-two-three-four; ONE-two-three-four) to awaken your fourth chakra. Keep drumming until you feel the power coming, and then join with it. Then stop drumming, and do the following breathing exercise:

227

From your base chakra, stream upward with your inhale until you reach your crown chakra; from there, flow out into the vast expanse of the sky, as if you are leaving your body with this breath. n the exhale, enter your body again, coming back from the universe, and sink down to the point where you contact the tree with your bottom or with your feet.

Continue this exercise until you can clearly feel how you are joined with infinity on each inhale, and feel your ties with your earthly, finite, material level on each exhale. This breathing exercise leads you into your axis between heaven and earth and opens the pathway that bridges the material and the immaterial world. You become the cosmic tree yourself, which is the center of the world within you and is the only point and position from where you can receive the power of the eternal stuff of life.

On the inhale, you receive from the wealth of ideas of the eternally creative spirit, and on the exhale, the ideas penetrate the material level and urge to be given gestalt and realization. While you are connected with the cosmic breath, ask which "cell" you represent within this cosmic organism, which function you have to fulfill for the Whole to be healthy. Stay in the tree as long as is necessary for you to be initiated into the next important step for your mission. Only then close the ritual with an expression of gratitude to all spirits. Breathe strongly a few times and climb down from the tree. Embrace it in gratitude and leave behind a little gift of tobacco.

The Morning and Evening Ceremonies

Starting and closing day and night in a ceremonial way reminds us that every day is special. In these ceremonies, we celebrate each day's uniqueness. Just to wake up in the morning is a great gift that we almost always ignore and take for granted. Unaware, we stumble into the day. No one knows what the day will bring, or if we will be allowed to see the evening, even though we act as though we know all that in advance.

To ceremonially start and close each day gives us the opportunity to proceed on our path step by step. Every day contains a necessary step for our growth, and we can afford to give it some thought in the morning and examine its fulfillment and realization in the evening by probing our conscience.

The morning and evening ceremonies can be celebrated communally—for example, with friends, family, the community you live in—or alone. The ceremonies described below are meant to be held alone, but can easily be converted into communal ceremonies.

The Morning Ritual

Upon waking up in the morning, try to bring your dream from the world of the nagual into the tonal world. The shamans know a way to do this, which is by not moving and remaining silent until the dream image is completely reassembled in our mind. They say that with every movement a piece of the dream fabric will be lost forever. Recall your dream, and watch it like a movie with your mental eye. If your dream does not give you back any image or memory, call the keepers of the dreams to help you find it. Be patient and do not give up too soon; your dream will come back if the keepers of the dream consider it important for your growth. Arise only after you have found the dream or have the distinct feeling that it will not be revealed again today.

If you have a yard, you can celebrate the new day outside. It is especially beautiful to see the sunrise at the same time. Otherwise, stay in your room, and sit in your medicine wheel (which you can quickly outline with symbols for the eight directions, if you do not have it permanently built) in the place of the west facing the birthplace of the morning, the east. Ritually cleanse yourself with smoke, and say a clear thank you to the Sun, the Great Father, for coming again to share his power of inspiration with you; thank him for the gift of the new day. If you would like to dedicate more time to this ceremony, here are six breathing exercises to wake up your body and bring it great pleasure. You must stand to do them, but keep facing east.

1. Breathe in strongly, and abruptly push the air into your third chakra; with another breath, push into the chest to the fourth chakra. Hold the air there until you feel the need to breathe out. Repeat five times.

2. Abruptly breathe in small amounts of air to strongly move diaphragm and peritoneum. Repeat a few times.

3. Small death breathing. Breathe in for the duration of twelve heartbeats, hold for twelve heartbeats, breathe out for twelve heartbeats and hold again for twelve beats. Repeat seven times.

4. On the inhale, raise your arms and hold your breath as long as possible, remaining in this tense position. Then completely let go on your exhale and collapse by letting your chest fall over and your arms touch the ground. Repeat three times.

5. "The lion's roar." Breathe in strongly and raise your arms; on the exhale, let your upper body drop to a horizontal position, stick out your head, swing your arms back, and let out a loud scream. Repeat three times.

6. Breathe in strongly, and on the exhale, form your lips as if you were blowing a trumpet and intermittently breathe out while making trumpetlike sounds.

After these exercises return to the place of the west and look east, to the power of the sun. Call or pray to this power, the power of light, enlightenment and inspiration, for it to illuminate the stretch of path you must walk today, to pervade today's steps with creative power and to let you walk on the earth in love.

Remember your dream from the night before, and take it as a message for today; pay attention to what it wants to tell you and meditate upon its contents: Does it show you pictures that unmistakably point to events that you will experience today? Is it interwoven with unfinished things from yesterday that weigh on you because you resisted them? Listen to today's task, to what you have to change or turn around for power to arise.

If you have received these instructions, call the power of the sacred Two, the power of the Earth, and request her to strengthen your will. Ask for this day to become a sacred day, and to let its ties with the Whole become transparent to everyone. If you like, you can sing your power song and dance your animal . . . and then devote yourself to your morning coffee.

During the ritual you may be given a certain theme for the day. If so, try to consider everything you do and everything that happens to you during the day from the perspective of this theme, so that all the events of the day can be related to one another, and, when considered as a whole, reveal the symbolic meaning of the theme.

The Evening Ritual

In the evening, before you go to sleep—or pass over into the realm of the nagual—you can close the day with a small ritual by dreaming your "day dream" again and ushering it into your night dream. Sit at the place of the southwest in your medicine wheel, the place of the dreams. Cleanse yourself with smoke and call the sacred powers. Reflect on the day.

What did it show you? Was it a happy day or a sorrowful day? Did you have any difficulties? Where did you meet any resistance, inner or outer? Which situations did you encounter with all your power? Did you experience anything new? Were you successful in integrating parts of your nightly dreams into your "day dream"? Did you fulfill the directions that you received during the morning ceremony? What were the hindrances? Did you live in the power of love? Was there anything you were unable to master? Which of the shields created difficulties for you today? Were you able to balance it with the power of another shield? Where did you become unbalanced? Did you feel as one with the power of your allies in any of these situations?

These questions will come to you by themselves; sometimes there will be only one and sometimes many. Be honest with yourself, try not to find excuses. If you come across a situation that is still not complete or if events of the day remained misunderstood, ask the guardians of your dreams to give you a key during the night.

If you know your allies, you can ask them too. Hold your power object over the respective chakra (for the ally in the realm of the stones it is the second chakra, for the plant ally it is the third chakra and for the animal ally it is the fourth chakra), and speak your question aloud trying to get an answer that way. This exercise must be done without any expectations, in innocence and trust. Sing your power song or dance your animal.

At the end, you can wake up your seventh chakra, your dream body, with the help of light-meditation. Lie down on the ground with your head in the southwest. With several breaths, send your concentrated awareness into the seventh chakra. On the inhale, absorb the power of the earth with your first chakra, send it up the spine and out through the crown chakra into the universe. On the exhale, visualize yourself coming back from the universe, riding on a white river of light, entering into the seventh chakra and letting the light flood your inner.

If you are familiar with crystal medicine, you can also balance your wheel of dreams holding a crystal, tip pointing downward, over your head and rotating it clockwise thirteen times. Thank the powers of the day and go to bed.

Here is another dream exercise that will teach you to consciously glide from your waking state over the threshold into sleep. With your eyes closed, visualize a mirror that reflects your own face. Try to see your face as clearly as possible. As soon as you have succeeded, go through the mirror. Another exercise is the following: close your eyes when you are in bed and visualize your hands. Concentrate with such intensity that you really start seeing your hands.

The most beautiful way, of course, is to try and create your own personal rituals. The ones described here are only meant to be suggestions and stimuli that you can use in the beginning. You can change or elaborate on these rituals once you have discovered your own style. There are no rules except that you have to be aware of what you are doing, and that what you are doing is sacred.

The Full Moon Ritual

In the same way the morning and evening ceremonies can help us join the natural rhythm and let ourselves resonate in the change from light into darkness, we can unite with the natural cycles of the moon by performing a full moon ritual. With every cycle of the moon we can reflect and ask ourselves: "Are there any parts in me that want to wax and grow? Are there any that want to wane and dwindle?" Link whatever wants to grow or dwindle with the powers of the medicine wheel, with the powers of the four directions that you have opened up through working with the four shields. Ask while sitting in the place of the respective shield what you need to do to bring it back into balance.

The full moon ceremony is celebrated at night, but if the moon will not be full until the daytime, perform it the night before, NEVER the night after the full moon. It is most proper to perform it under the open sky, either alone or with others. Create a circle with the eight directions, or use your medicine wheel if you have one outdoors. Dedicate the site by cleansing it with the smoke of the sacred herbs, call the holy powers and request them to come to the center of your circle. Cleanse all participants with smoke in the circle. Call the power of the moon and ask it to be with you. A drum or rattle can be used in a 3/4 beat (ONE-two-three, ONE-two-three) to tune everyone in. It will help all participants open to the lunar power and will help them to absorb it with their third chakra. Meditation begins with everyone looking at the shining disk of the moon, followed by a cycle of prayers. Everyone puts their concerns out in the open, reveals whatever wants to grow or disappear within them, and promises the moon that they will join it during its cycle, waxing and waning with it.

Once all have prayed, the charging with lunar power begins. Everyone takes turns coming to the center of the circle, closing their eyes. The others now walk clockwise around the person in the center, to charge him or her with lunar power. Scoop up lunar energy with your left hand and bring it to the one who stands in the center; the right hand is behind the left, pushing it forward. After seventeen rotations (the sacred Seventeen is the power which complements the sacred Three becoming the sacred Twenty), the next person goes to the center. (If you are celebrating this ceremony in a permanent wheel you cannot stand directly in the center because it may never be touched. Stand at the place of the sacred Five instead.)

When you are charged with lunar energy, there is a distinct physical feeling: You think you are actually growing in size, and you can feel the energy flowing around your body like a spiraling mantle of power. For all gestures to be conscious and powerful, each participant should be aware of what is occurring in this ritual. After charging, everyone returns to their seats in the circle.

Now, the leader of the ceremony (perhaps you if you are leading the ceremony) picks up a vessel of water that has been kept in a dedicated spot, inside or out, a day ahead of the ceremony to absorb lunar energy, and place it in front of your third chakra. Hold the container with your left hand. Your right should be held just above the glass with the palm facing down. Breathe in deeply three times, becoming a conscious channel, so permeable that the lunar power can travel right through you and out of your right hand into the water.

This will magnetize the water and dedicate it with the energy of the moon. Pass the vessel around for everyone to drink from. To complete the ritual, all participants join hands to form a circle of energy. Concentrate on receiving energy from the right hand of your partner on your left, and send it out of your right hand into the left hand of the partner on your right. After some time, you will be able to feel the ever increasing circulation of the current of energy. This energy can be mentally transmitted to someone in need. Visualize the person concerned as standing right in front of you, and pass this energy that is streaming through you to that person. A song to the moon or a prayer in gratitude closes the ritual.

Another method enabling you to absorb the power of the moon is by practicing the following chakra meditation:

Begin by feeling yourself drawn into the silence of your body at the point of the base chakra, the first lightbody, where you sit touching the ground. Then, on the inhale, pull up the power of the earth and go to the second chakra. On the exhale, push it back to the base chakra. Proceed in this way until you have reached the seventh chakra, then stream up and down with your breath from the base to the crown a few times, and, when you feel the energy flowing freely, take the reverse route: While breathing in, take power from the moonlight and pull it into your seventh chakra. On the exhale, remain there and let it dissipate. On the next inhale, pull in the power of the moon and channel it into the sixth chakra via the seventh and let it dissipate there on the exhale. Proceed in this way until you reach the base chakra again. Then flow with your breath into your base chakra, coming down from the crown which is now connected to the power of the moon. Become aware of the moonlight, and see how it streams into you!

Lunar energy has other shamanic uses. If you are working with objects of power, it is a good idea to expose them to the moon's light, either all night long if you find a safe place for them, or just for the duration of the ceremony. Take the opportunity to meditate on your power objects. Handle them one by one and be reminded of their medicines and connection with you.

The days after a full moon are the best time to let go of illnesses, physical pains and other disharmonies. It is best to visit a tree for this purpose. The appropriate ritual has been described earlier.

In connection with the lunar ritual, let us talk about an ancient custom known to the Celts and the Germanic tribes:

They wore a lunar amulet, called a Torc. It was massive, made of silver or gold, and was worn as a ring around the neck, sometimes having a lunar "barge" in the center. This lunar amulet served as protection against the high-voltage energy that prevails around the times of the full and new moon.

The precious metals gold and silver have the ability to screen out radiation if it becomes too strong for humans. Our forebears knew that moon and earth have the same electric polarity. They may not have known that they are negatively charged, but they could feel how both earth and moon attract the electricity of the sun, especially when the moon is positioned between earth and sun (new moon) or when it is behind the earth as seen from the sun (full moon).

Today, scientists and physicians have investigated the moon's influence on human beings and on the entire earthly growth process, removing this idea from the realm of superstition. It has also been proved that sensitivity to lunar influences is not imaginary—it is caused by increased electricity coming from the sun, shrinking the capillaries in the human body, and reducing overall circulation. The effects are felt as difficulty in concentrating, as headaches and fatigue. Some are subject to "lunar moods," being easily irritated and having disturbed sleep or no sleep.

In days of yore, the lunar amulet was worn three days before and three days after the full moon, helping the people of that time remain safe from these high-voltage energy fields. This makes it a meaningful piece of jewelry to wear today for personal protection and maintenance of health. You can have one custom made to your specifications, or you can make it yourself.

Another possibility for enhancing the lunar ceremony is to include the "spiral medicine" because it has a harmonizing effect on human energy, keeping it in balance in spite of the increased tension of the moonlight. Your creativity need not know any bounds in shaping your lunar ceremony; the only important thing is that everything you create should be related to the Whole, to the ritual.

If you choose to celebrate the ritual described above, you should be aware of the waxing cycle of the moon until it reaches fullness. Accompany the waning phase of the moon with the waning of your "inner moon" by consciously reducing and letting go of everything that you have promised on the full moon day. Then you can ritually bury it in the ground or burn it in a fire during a ceremony on the no-moon day. In its waxing phase, accompany it with your "inner waxing" while remembering your promise from the last full moon celebration and really try to fulfill it. During the next full moon ritual you can meditate on this cycle and the fulfillment of your promises.

The Birthday Ritual

Vision Quest at the Beginning of a New Year in Life

The birthday ceremony must be performed alone, in the all-oneness of the cosmic powers. If you are celebrating it for the first time, ask a friend to accompany you as your protector and body-guard, so to speak. The ceremony starts the night before your birthday. You need to take with you all the items and power objects in your medicine bag, a drum and rattle, your burning dish with herbs and feather, tobacco, sweet liqueur, some perfume, perhaps

237

a compass to determine the sacred directions and a cigarette lighter or matches.

During the preparations, think of an object that best represents the most important event in your life of the past year. Bring this object along also. Set out in the late afternoon to a place in a wilderness area where you can be undisturbed for an entire night and where you can also make a fire. If you take along a guardian, you should not talk to each other. Become absorbed into the language of nature, and let yourself be guided to the right spot. Once you have found it, build your medicine wheel. It is enough to mark the eight directions with eight stones and and to have the fire marking the center. Once you have laid out the circle, collect enough firewood for one night. Do not forget to be respectful, thankful and humble when you collect the wood and stones.

After you have collected everything, dedicate the circle and invoke the sacred powers requesting them to join you and sanctify the circle. You and your guardian cleanse each other with smoke, then cleanse your objects. Ask your friend to stay out of sight but within calling distance should you need help. When the sun begins to set, you should be ready to enter your medicine wheel. Sit in the place of the west and look into the setting sun. In the same way that the sun's light vanishes, a year in your life draws to a close. Think of the fullness of the year in retrospect: What was your harvest? What did it mean for your medicine? Contemplate on the object that represents the most important event or vision in your life this year, and remember its message. With the object in your hand, go to the north of the wheel and meditate there on how you have integrated its message into your medicine. Decide whether you can give this message and its symbolic power back to the earth, so you can be empty again and ready for a new step. If you are willing to let go of it, then bury it in the ground, with gratitude, to the west of the center of your wheel.

Now the second part of the ceremony begins. You have said good-by to whatever is past—it is integrated into you as a transforming power, has become knowledge and wisdom, increasing your medicine, and now you can face nothingness again, the unknown, for whose vision you pray. Now sit in the east of the circle, the place of the power of inspiration and vision. Use your drum and rattle and call all the particular powers with all your might and ask them from the bottom of your heart that they grant your vision quest for the coming year with signs and directions—now, this night! With each beat of the drum meditate on the power that you are calling: your helpers in the realms of the animals, plants and stones; the power of your medicine allies; the power of those ancestors and relatives who had been close to you and gave you a sense of direction by the way they mastered their own lives. If you call the power of dreams, remember the great dreams that inspired you this past year. Ask all the forces to become sources of power, to become sources of light; to illuminate the darkness of the coming year that lies before you like an empty land; and to reveal to you what you must do to make this piece of soil productive. Let your eyes scan the darkness of the night again and again. Try to send your awareness out in all four directions so you can perceive through the powers of your four shields anything that might contain an answer from the sacred entities of the universe.

You might receive a tonal answer: A particular animal may enter the circle from one of the eight directions; an owl or nighthawk may circle in a definite direction or directly above your wheel; the call of a nocturnal bird may support one of your prayers or address a specific concern; a bolt of lightning or sheet lightning might be seen in a certain direction; a sudden breeze might blow from a certain direction; a glowworm could sit on one of the stones.

You might receive a nagual answer in the form of the spirit of an ancestor or saint, of mythological figures or of spiritual entities. Sometimes frightening things can happen: Dark shadows might rush toward you, these being generally projections of your own fears that have come forth from their hiding places into the open. This provides an opportunity for you to encounter them face to face and to overcome them once and for all. View them now from a different perspective, see them as something other than fearful and unreal emotions, confront them with a shield other than that of the childish southern shield with its lost trust.

Shamans maintain that in reality there is no fear; it is only a figment of our imagination, and completely alien to nature. This is why in the first trial of their apprenticeship, shamans must face their fears to erase this unreal world of appearances. They have to learn to dance with their fears, which means avoiding seeing them from a fixed point of view. They take them by the arm like a friend, and dance with them around the medicine wheel, seeing them from all perspectives. This teaches the novices to meet their fears in the power of Oneness which says: "There is only love."

If something frightens you on first sight during your nightwatch, try not to let yourself be immediately pushed into your child-shield of the south; do not call your bodyguard for help immediately. Try to remember that you are seated in a sacred space, one that protects you with the power of its Wholeness, one to help you overcome and transform your fear into trust. Go into those fears and shadows and become aware of the delusions they evoke. Call on your allies; for example, dance your power animal and let its power take over your body so you can scrutinize those shadowy beings through its eyes. Or take a drum and join the sacred Three, the power of trust, beating a 3/4 rhythm (ONE-two-three, ONE-two-three). Always let yourself be guided—the sacred wheel will not desert you and will give you hints about which power you should join with to fight this battle successfully. It is a wonderfully powerful feeling when you see how this fear has been transformed into strength and the shadows are now transformed into light. If you have managed this, the night has given you a precious gift.

Now, start the fire in the center of your wheel. While you are doing this, talk to your relatives the wood and the herbs that you put into the fire, and talk to the flames themselves. Sing and beat the drum to the spirit of the fire; call upon it, and put your whole heart, love and gratitude into this performance. Set the fire into a favorable mood by your prayers, with sacrifices (of the herbs and perfume), and with your music and dance so it will favorably accept you. Its acceptance will be shown by letting you put your hands into it without harm. Bring the power of the fire to your chakras again and again, cleansing and harmonizing them, making them channels for the world of the nagual.

Never allow your awareness to lapse; this night should be celebrated as wide awake and completely as possible. All the signs that are given to you are gifts from the powers for your medicine. Take everything that is given into your heart and allow it to mature into an image that will give meaning and direction for the new year. A new ally could be revealed, or a vision could provide fresh inspiration for the starting of a new profession, perhaps a hint could be given on how to change a troubled relationship with a friend or maybe an insight showing the current meaning of an illness. The darkness of this night will fade with the onset of dawn, yet the magic will remain and the outpouring of the morning sun's rays will usher in your new year.

Be sure and thank the sacred powers of the site, the fire, all the helping spirits and allies. Quiet the energy of the site by sprinkling water and sweet liqueur on it. Call to your friend and thank him or her for helping you. Go home together where your friends await you with a birthday sweat lodge that enables you to share the vision of the previous night with them.

Daily Life—A Celebration

The ceremonies that we have discussed are only a few selected from the abundance of rituals that life showers on us. Though it may be a great help to create and perform rituals, the real power of a ceremony is only complete if we are able to actualize it in our daily lives and not simply let it evaporate once completed. If we carry out all our small and great duties in the full awareness of the powers of our four shields and understand them in connection with the superior Whole, every action, work and movement becomes a ceremonial celebration through which we express and respect the beauty of the earth. Once we stop living out of old habits and start seeing with eyes that know no yesterday and no tomorrow, eyes that are able to vividly see the Now, in which the fullness of life keeps touching us unexpectedly, always fresh, in which we are shown every step of the path we take toward the strengthening of our medicine, then we will be able to send our excessive need for planning and security back to where it belongs—beyond the four directions. The power of trust will guide us to this Now.

Nobody can say for sure what the next hour will bring—we do not even know if we will be able to live through it. We do not know if we will ever see that friend we are talking to right now ever again; whether our house will still be there when we come home from work; we do not know if our spouse will be there as usual(!); we do not know if the sun will be willing to illuminate a new morning.

In spite of all these uncertainties we pretend that we know what will happen, simply because it has always been this way—that we are used to it. Every experience that goes beyond the scope of our habits can surprise us to such an extent that we can become completely unbalanced. If we are willing to accept the uniqueness of each day, hour and minute and see no difference between every day and Sun-day, to realize that every day is sunny, inspired and stimulated by the eternal power of existence in the Here and Now, we can celebrate life as a service to God, an eternal celebration in unison with heaven and earth.

To comprehend our life as a ceremony is to understand macrocosmic reality as a metaphor for our microcosmic existence. To transform our uprootedness and separation from universal Oneness into the unifying power of the Whole, we must be careful not to erect new barriers in our work with the medicine wheel by separating our actions and exercises from our everyday life. It must not become a hobby or an ambition that makes us hungry for power. The most sophisticated and difficult spiritual exercise is the realization and celebration of our divine service in our daily lives. Awakening is a prerequisite. It is all right to fall back into old habits and experience defeat; what is important is our commitment and courage to wake up again. Here are the quotations of two awakened souls:

> Man is fundamentally at risk
> Defeat harms him less than so-called security.
> God does not want seekers of metaphysical emergency exits,
> but perfectors of human existence
> from the material to the transcendental.
>
> (Herbert Fritsche)

> Only the one who fully comprehends the difficulties of awakening can understand that long and arduous work is needed to wake up.
>
> (G. Gurdjeff)

PART V

THE EIGHT YEARLY SOLAR CELEBRATIONS OF THE EARTH

"We live on earth to celebrate our life in unison with the universe."

These are the words of an Indian shaman. The eight celebrations of the sun are the celebrations of the eight directions of the Medicine Wheel. Through them, mankind as a species celebrates its unity with the universe.

To observe the eight celebrations of the Sun in light of their original power and purity, we must return again to our early Stone Age heritage. Our Stone Age ancestors knew themselves to be a part of the Great Cosmic Family. Everyone understood themselves to be children of Sun and Earth and worshiped them as their Great Parents, who gave and sustained life so long as they were heeded. Instinctively, everyone knew their bodily axis was their connecting point with Heaven and Earth. They had to remain in this axis to be able to receive the vision that the Great Father tirelessly bestowed, and to dance it awake as His dream on Earth, the Great Mother. In their Great Parents they had two wonderful helpers who allowed them to discover the Oneness of Heaven and Earth.

The Earth, in its loving dance around its partner the Sun, experiences a special meeting with its Beloved eight times a year. This is essential for its own growth and development of consciousness, and all life on earth is affected by these meetings as well: the tides of the year and the rhythms of nature, all growing, maturing and dying. These meetings are the power of the spiral of light, drawing its eternal circles, while aiming the infinitely finite powers of the nagual like fiery arrows at the Earth.

Our early Stone Age ancestors felt the ups and downs of these time waves. They pulsated with the vibrating breath of their Earth

Mother, and together with her were immersed in the eightfold impulses of the Sun, the eternally circulating light. Through this essential relationship they felt as One with their Great Parents, and the fertile High Times were the occasions to celebrate together.

What is the significance of these eight celebrations for us today? It is the time of rediscovering our connection with the Great Family. (The Eight Sun Festivals of the Earth are primordial religious celebrations, showing devotion and open worship that constitute our Circle of Visions.) It is the fundamental image of Man, shown to us by the Medicine Wheel: it is a way to see ourselves interwoven into the Great Mother's circle of vision. In our development of consciousness—from the sacred Five to the sacred Twenty—we are all connected with the universe through the eight directions. These powers are arrows pointing to the center. Every day and every hour we are dancing with them—sometimes a little more intensely with the power of the south, sometimes more with the power of the north.

A grand and unique aspect of the eight celebrations is that at these times of the year the whole of humanity and the Earth align their "wheels" with the Sun. Human beings and the Earth become subject to the same themes displayed by the eight directions of the Wheel, and come into harmony as like-minded beings. We are able to clarify our essential relationship with the Sun and Earth and enhance our relationship with the natural cycles, which become a mirror for our inner rhythms. Borne by the power of natural rhythms, we can become "normal" again. We can let go of our displaced positions, and reintegrate ourselves within the Cosmic Family where we all know what we really are—medicine women and medicine men!

Today we are still the children of Sun and Earth, even though it may sound childish to our intellectualized ears. It is a primeval cosmic image that is valid for the entire human race for eternity. The Sun, as the power of light and vision, always was and still is the symbol of the totality of human consciousness—it is the bearer of consciousness. The Sun's paternal legacy for our part in human existence lies in a certain task, our dream. It will reward us with inspiration for its earthly fulfillment whenever we turn to him in vision quest. If we join the Earth and accompany her in intimate understanding on her yearly journey around the sun, pausing eight times at the points of the eight directions, we can grasp with her whatever specific impulse of light energy the Sun showers upon us at these stations.

If the eight solar festivals are celebrated in accordance with precise astrological/astronomical data, we can experience the concentrated power of the nagual. We can open up to it more easily on these occasions than at other times because the Sun is more in tune with one of the eight directions.

Some of the early Christian church festivals derived from the four cardinal meetings of Sun and Earth (solstices and equinoxes) have retained their original character.

Let us start with the lowest point of the Sun as seen from Earth's northern hemisphere. It is the longest night of the year, the Winter Solstice on the twenty-first of December, around Christmastime. The Sun journeys upward again from there, and after three months it reaches the Equinox on the twenty-first of March, the beginning of Spring, the original time of Easter. Another three months later, on the twenty-first of June, the Sun reaches its highest point; it is the longest day of the year, the Summer Solstice, the time of the Festival of John the Baptist. From there the Sun descends again until light and darkness are equal, the Autumnal Equinox on the twenty-third of September. On this day Thanksgiving for the fall harvest was originally celebrated.

The rhythmic celebration of these Four Festivals is still common practice. But few members of the various religions are aware of the original meaning of these festivals as they were originally celebrated by the child-man of the early Stone Age. Just the consideration of the four cardinal festivals of the Sun will reveal their significance. Let us consider the succession of the seasons.

The gentle knocking of Spring brings the first colors after the silence and scarcity of winter. Then Summer bursts in with its overpowering wealth of bold paintings and scorching heat, just to throw itself into the arms of its brother Autumn, who pours his horn of plenty onto the land. In silent melancholy Autumn sings the song of death into the wind until it swells to a howl and all forms and shapes disappear into nebulous realms and brother Winter appears and throws a white blanket over everything.

Images like this can help us give form and meaning to the four celebrations. If we supplement the four major festivals with the four minor festivals, we get the circle of the eight celebrations as shown in the illustration.

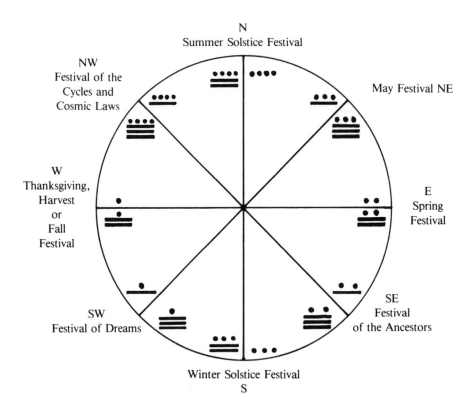

For the descriptions of the eight festivals I have relied entirely upon the wisdom of the Medicine Wheel and inspiration from Nature. We could probably find different starting points. The Chinese, for example, continued to maintain the heritage of the Stone Age and the tradition of the Eight Festivals of the Sun until the revolution in 1911. For this reason it is possible to consult the *I Ching or Book of Changes*, for the organization of the eight festivals. Astrology can also be a source of information. The festival times will manifest themselves differently due to natural occurrances, of course, depending where one is on the earth, for example, the poles or the southern hemisphere, but we are going to consider them from the European and North American standpoint.

We celebrate the Eight Festivals according to the natural movement of the Earth around the Sun, counterclockwise. Through this cyclic motion of the Earth around the Sun we become its eternal children. Together with our Great Mother we wear our festive clothes and decorate ourselves and our homes and communities, and make our way to the "services" that the whole of humanity is invited to, in the Spirit of the Sun.

◀ 21st of December ▶
The Celebration of the South

We will start our tour of the Festivals with the natural beginning of the year, the Winter Solstice on the twenty-first of December. The Holy Night is the longest night of the year. The Earth and all life on it are immersed in the deepest darkness of the year, the amorphous blackness, the audible silence of the cosmic obscurity. Courageously, the Earth Mother surrenders to the secret of the longest night; she withdraws entirely into her own darkness, concentrates on her own depths to dream in the realm of the not-yet-revealed and gathers the necessary strength for her next cycle.

This primordial gesture of the Great Mother is a symbol for the child-man whom we know from the Epic of Gilgamesh, the godlike enlightened one, who must descend into his own depths, into his own darkness of the soul, to meet his brother Enkidu who is the black shadow. Everyone loves Gilgamesh, who shines like the Sun and wants to avoid Enkidu, his gloomy brother. But both are halves of the whole man, and both have to unite to become one—because where there is light, there is also shadow. We can only understand and comprehend light if we think darkness at the same time. Brother Enkidu is celebrated by the childlike being in the South of the Medicine Wheel.

The South, with the power of the sacred Three and Thirteen, joins the soul of Man with the Power of the Plants and the Realm of Water. Our familiar custom of erecting a green tree at Christmas and decorating it with lights reminds us of this. We are reminded of innocence and trust displayed by the plants during this Festival: In the same way that they as seeds feel safe in surrendering to the darkness of the Earth and feel that it is their source of growth that will lead them to the light, we as people have to immerse ourselves into the abysmal darkness of the soul, into the dark waters of the sea of our emotions and trust that our surrender to the darkness will lead us to light.

This is the real gift of this night: the rebirth of light. The longest night of the year proclaims the departure of darkness and greets the first reborn rays of light. We are celebrating Christ, who is given to us by the Universe in this night as a newborn and innocent child of light to illuminate the darkness. During this Festival we share with the Earth and all its creatures the recovered light in the spirit of Love and Peace. The light's first subtle rays penetrate the dark cave of our inner being and help us answer the questions: "What seed will germinate and grow in me this year? What responsibilities must I bear, which sorrows, that I may grow in harmony with Everything? Where do I confront my light and dark sides? Which part in me is Gilgamesh and which part Enkidu?"

We also meet Heraclitus, an honored guest in our Inner, because we have undergone the Twelve Trials of the twelve months in heroic fashion. We may set out on our new yearly adventure with freshly gathered strength, without false humility, as heroes. This adventure, a plan still without form, lies before us as a wealth of opportunities. Our soul discovers something sacred and healing in this night. It is in Harmony, and we keep the peace of this night like shepherds and share our joy by giving and receiving gifts.

◀ 4th of February ▶
The Celebration of the Southeast

Let us accompany the Earth for one and a half months on its path around the Sun, and pause to celebrate the Festival of the Ancestors, the Celebration of the sacred Six and Sixteen. It is still Winter, but with the days slowly getting longer, we have premonitions of Springtime. We start to have notions of Life Forces unfolding beneath the snowy blanket of Winter. We intuit the busy hands of our Great Mother preparing to reveal themselves. We can see the first sprouts breaking through the surface of the Earth to absorb their first sunlight. All the forces of Nature start about their business.

We too are called upon to join the work of our Cosmic Family. Our Ancestors encourage us to do just that. On this day they talk to us, and we can ask them for help. With their light they illuminate our boldest ideas and utopian dreams. They help us to realize and actualize them, so that we can give them back to the Universe as our contribution to the Divine Plan. On this day we meet the Ancestors and understand that they are the Enlightened Ones. We should remember one Ancestor in particular, recall his or her work and contribution, and meet this Ancestor on the Bridge of the

Nagual to illuminate the question: "What is it that links my light with yours?"

During this Festival we join the Earth's dream of the future, that we will participate in it as her Children—we bear the responsibility for its realization. We are instruments and serving assistants who are having fun working and creating, who enjoy unfolding our talents and gifts, and want to make meaningful contributions to the Whole.

◀ 21st of March ▶
The Celebration of the East

We are a month and a half farther along in our journey with the Earth around the Sun; we adorn ourselves anew and learn the rhythm and rhyme of another festive dance, the Celebration of the Appearance of Spring.

Day and Night are equal. We celebrate the resurrected light that becomes visible in the longer days. We start blooming with the first flowers and take responsibility for ourselves and everything that happens in our ripening process. The Great Mother's special message for us on this day is showing us how she receives the power of fire and creativity and transforms them into her own source of power. During this celebration, the Sun gives us his fire to kindle our visions. And his fire teaches us that something must die first in order to be reborn, that the death of matter gives birth to light.

As Children of the Sun we are ourselves creators—by vision and by orgasm. During this Festival we ask for our personal vision, for direction regarding the next steps that we are about to take. It is a festival of revelation, a message of the Sun, the Song of Songs of the immortal and eternal spirit which proclaims the divine, the creative universal spirit.

Together with the Earth and all its creatures, we discover our own resurrection through our passion and surrender to the bursting open of all Life. We ourselves are the blazing bonfires of Easter, the lamb with the banner of victory, enlightened by hanging from the cross, initiates into the mysteries of death and birth.

◀ 6th of May ▶
The Festival of the Northeast

Another month and a half later we make garlands of flowers and circle the Maytree to decorate it and dance around it. Pan, the horned god, makes an appearance for this dance. He leads the ball and opens our senses to tune us in to the sound of the Earth. We become one with the essence of the stone, plant and animal; we become intoxicated by the wealth of shapes and forms around us, and luxuriate in enchantment at the well-rounded bosom of the Great Goddess Earth who receives her Beloved on this day and celebrates Walpurgis Night in a transport of the senses and earthly love, to give life anew. Heaven and Earth love each other and let us take part in their feast, so that we may discover healing in the Oneness of all beings.

The pulsating sap of Life from the Maytree reaches over and touches us, and we feel its current, its upward surge from the roots to the crown; our arteries throb in unison, and its healing green of life envelops us like a coat of leaves. We have come with our Medicine Shields, to place them on the Maytree to display and share them with all our Companions in the Dance. The Power of Motion, the powers of the Nagual, the sacred Nine and Nineteen come to us in this Celebration. They shower us from their horn of plenty to move our medicine, to transform it more and more into a healing elixir—one that will beautify the Earth. Our Four Shields become round; we dance with them and balance their four lights in all Four Directions.

The contact with our older brothers and sisters, the stones, plants and animals, enable us to dive into the world of matter. We listen to the vibrations and sounds of their language; we smell their scents and taste the composition of their Work. The splendor of colors around us streams into our bodies and lets its light shine like a rainbow that arches across Heaven and Earth.

◀ 21st of June ▶
The Festival of the North

Together with the growing light, we journey another month and a half around the Sun, and on the longest day of the year we celebrate the Summer Solstice. It is the Festival of the North, because there will be no night in the north of the Earth, for the Sun will shine there for twenty-four hours. Here the secret of the Sun is revealed and says: "Behold, as you see me now, throughout the round of day and night, so am I with you always, even if you cannot see me." With the Light of the Summer everything hidden comes to blossom. The highest point of the Sun fills us with the power of the animal Spirits. It helps us to enlighten our heart so we can set our inner animal free so that its instinct, its clarity of action and knowledge may take hold of our minds. We light the bonfires that burn all night like the Sun in the North, and purify ourselves by thrusting all our false thinking into the flames. Through this purification, our Higher Self bursts from its cocoon, our lower Self, and shines in the center of the Heavens like the Pole Star in which all knowledge, logic and power of mind are integrated.

We start to respect and love our roles and those of others; if we call the sacred Four and Fourteen for help—they talk to us directly on this day. We throw off our ego and unite with our animal nature and with our ally from the realm of the animals, who will give us direction during this descent into the ensuing darkness. For the Sun must leave his lofty throne and descend into the depths of the dark realm. Thus, at the sun's highest point, we are celebrating the reappearance of darkness.

◀ 8th of August ▶
The Festival of the Northwest

Again, one and a half months later, we bring ourselves into tune with the Earth through the Festival of the Cycles and Cosmic Laws. We unite with the power of the sacred Eight which comes to us from the world of the plants. Plants remind us of their primary trust in the cycles and laws of nature; they know their essential needs and live in harmony because they know they will be satisfied. We think of our emotions and motives, the essential things that nourish our growth. We can discover them through dialogue with our plant Ally.

Prepared in this way we receive the power of the sacred Eight, the finite but still infinitely recurring cycles. Our feet follow the outline of an eight while dancing. We dance and dance; we feel the point of contact of both circles, leaving behind whatever is fulfilled and swinging into whatever must be completed. Thus we walk through the gate between Death and Birth, and, heeding this rhythm, we discover the sacred Eight and the sacred Eighteen: the power of the Law Givers.

On this day they illumine the laws of our fate which we can accept joyously like the plants, if we have understood the law of the sacred Eight as a natural, primeval, Everlasting Law on which all growth is based. In the light of these powers it may be possible for us to live in peace and harmony with our own needs and those of others, like stones, plants, animals and each other.

◀ 23rd of September ▶
The Festival of the West

The light of the Sun proclaims the onset of Fall on this day. Day and Night are equal again. We celebrate the Harvest Festival. We march through the harvested fields and pastures of our Great Mother decorated with the fruits of the year, ready for consecration, inviting us to join the Thanksgiving feast. Everything that happened to us during this year has born fruit—grown, ripened and nourished by the constant change of light and darkness.

We look on our Harvest in retrospect—the material, mental and spiritual gifts that we received during this Year. The prime gesture of our Earth Mother during this Festival is the presenting and distributing of her fruits. We are touched by this gesture and release others from debt and guilt. We unburden ourselves from these material and emotional weights, to create fallow land within us, empty fields, ready to receive again.

As Day and Night are in balance during this festival, giving and taking should likewise be in a harmonious state of equilibrium. This is what our gift of sharing is all about. Around the Tree of Life the four fires of the Sacred Directions are blazing. Here we offer up our gifts, let them go, and their flames kindle our will again to sow, grow, give and take anew. The fear of Death and letting go is transformed in the fire and becomes the power of will, ready for new life. We sink to Earth with the falling leaves; the smells of dying foliage and the darkening colors accompany us on our journey into the inner world, where we withdraw to contemplate.

◀ 8th of November ▶
The Festival of the Southwest

The Nights that are constantly growing longer tune us into the festival of the sacred Seven and Seventeen, the celebration of the Dream and its Keepers. Insight into the realm of the dream is only granted by the Earth. The Great Mother shares her dream-weaving helpers with us: the Elemental Spirits of Fire, Water, Earth and Air; the salamanders and fauns, gnomes, dwarfs and devas, the undines, nymphs and wallines, the fairies, sylphs and trolls. They are the Spirits who guide us in the realm of dreams, host us as welcome guests with images and miracles, and nourish us with timeless and eternal light in endless space.

During this Celebration we are the hosts who lay the table filled with the favorite foods of the dream spirits: glittering ribbons, shimmering coins, colorful rings and small wreaths. We sprinkle the Earth with sweet liqueur and thank the spirits for their help by singing soft melodies. We bring with us a Dream that desires to become Reality, one we want to dance awake and dream visibly on Earth.

With this Dream, we go to one of the invisible helpers and ask for his or her light to release the Medicine of this Dream. Something inside of us understands that the Earth sends this Helper to us because it needs us to act as Architects to transform light into matter. This is our True Mission. The Earth Mother reminds us during this festival that we can only cross the threshold between dream and reality with the mediation of the Spirits of the Dreams, and only through our cooperation with them can we keep alive the bond between both Worlds.

After the mists of November, during the Advent season, we prepare ourselves again to celebrate the rebirth of light from its darkest night. Here our roundelay closes: One year is complete and the End is already pregnant with a new Beginning.

SHAMANIC HEALING

To the Spirit of
the Book

I depart from you now, and send you out
to the unknown, to those who will find you.
My companion you have been for one whole year;
you were my friend and my enemy as well.
You were my battle and my dance;
you were my shadow and my light,
my medicine, sometimes sweet, sometimes bitter.
You led me into foreign lands
where desert, mountain and rocks built borders,
where silence spoke to me
and darkness burst into light.
You led me often to the Source
forming drops of water into words,
that ran dry for one whole cycle of the moon
and revealed my emptiness to me.
But again it was filled
in the spirit of will and inspiration:
New sprouts grew, born from a long night's dream,
nourished in the vigil with the sacred stones,
that circled 'round me in their eightfold fashion.
With your help, spirits of this earth,
page after page I wove.
With you, foremost in mind, my beloved,
I examined the pillars of my constructs.
Lucecilla, Citrine, Mistela,
spirit of the owls and crystal of the mountain,
Fairy of the flute and blackbird,
you were true helpers to me!
Thank you, all my teachers
enrichers of my dreams.

260

TO THE SPIRIT OF THE BOOK

Now I let you go, my book,
harvest of my island year,
go on your way.
I let you travel.

I am empty once again,
and I hope to see you soon.

Extended Contents

EXTENDED CONTENTS

Index

— NOTES —

— NOTES —